TO THE LONG POND

To the Long Pond

The Adventures of an Evacuee

Ken Regelous

The Larks Press

Published by the Larks Press
Ordnance Farmhouse
Guist Bottom, Dereham, NR20 5PF
01328 829207

Printed by the Lanceni Press
Garrood Drive, Fakenham, Norfolk
01328 851578

British Library Cataloguing-in-Publication Data
A catalogue record for this book is available from
the British Library

Cover pictures
Front: The long Pond in 1996 (Photo by the author)
Back: Houses in Townshend Terrace reflected in the Lily Pond
with fish visible (Photo by Neville Tunmore)
Evacuation label and suitcase (Photo by the author)

ISBN 0 948400 82 X

ABOUT THE AUTHOR

After his time in King's Lynn, Ken Regelous went on to serious study and collected a number of academic qualifications including a Ph.D. in Philosophy and Sociology from Nottingham University. He later taught French and Mathematics in both state and private schools and lectured in sociology and philosophy in teacher training. He spent an important three years of his life in France, in a town with many waterways. He has worked as a correspondence tutor for the National Extension College for over 20 years ('the most pleasant and rewarding work I have ever done for pay' he says). He is the author of *Education Revisited* a development of the theories of John Rawls. Ken is married and has two sons, one a geologist and the other an environmentalist. He now owns a 30-acre organic farm in South Pembrokeshire.

Acknowledgements

The author wishes to thank the Lynn Museum, Lynn Library and True's Yard for their help in the preparation of this book. Thanks are also due to the Lynn News for permission to use old photographs and cuttings on pages 4, 5, 17, 25, 97, 160, & 161.
Neville Tunmore was most helpful, especially in the recollection of names, and the help of my wife, Rosemary, in reading and correcting, has been invaluable.

CONTENTS

New World	*1*
September 1st, 1940	*2*
Early Days	*8*
The Long Pond	*12*
The Key	*15*
Sandbagging	*16*
My Ditch	*18*
What's in a Name?	*19*
Winter in the Country	*22*
Old School Ties	*24*
Canes	*27*
Those Foreigners	*30*
First Day at the Long Pond	*34*
Henry Goes	*39*
Don't Want to Go Home?	*41*
My Ditch Filled In	*41*
Changing Schools	*43*
Worms	*43*
The Flea that Gave Itself Up	*46*
First One-day Wonder	*47*
The Pike	*50*
Relative Affluence	*51*
Country Activities	*55*
Long Pond Games	*57*
Comic Story	*61*
Look! No Bait!	*63*
Transferred	*65*
A Bike	*65*
Eeling with Sam Sutton	*67*
Littl'uns and Big'uns	*70*
The Long Pond Cast	*74*
Peter	*76*
Dead-eye	*79*
Stamps	*81*
Mansford Street Central	*84*
Glorious Mud	*91*
Scrumping	*93*
Wartime Lynn	*95*
In the Water	*101*
Trespassers	*104*

Dogs	*107*
Rivals to the Long Pond	*110*
Hosts of Problems	*113*
Big'uns that Got Away	*116*
Galloping Horses	*117*
Rendez-vous for Chat	*124*
Hedgelaying	*126*
Brief Call	*127*
Long Pond Characters	*129*
Old Ken	*133*
Ponded!	*136*
Bottomless Well	*141*
Neville Tunmore	*143*
To the Rescue	*146*
Cats	*147*
Mystery Man	*149*
Lend a Hand on the Land	*151*
Paradise Lost	*152*
Re-evacuated	*157*
Epilogue	*160*

The waterways of the Long Pond and district in 1939

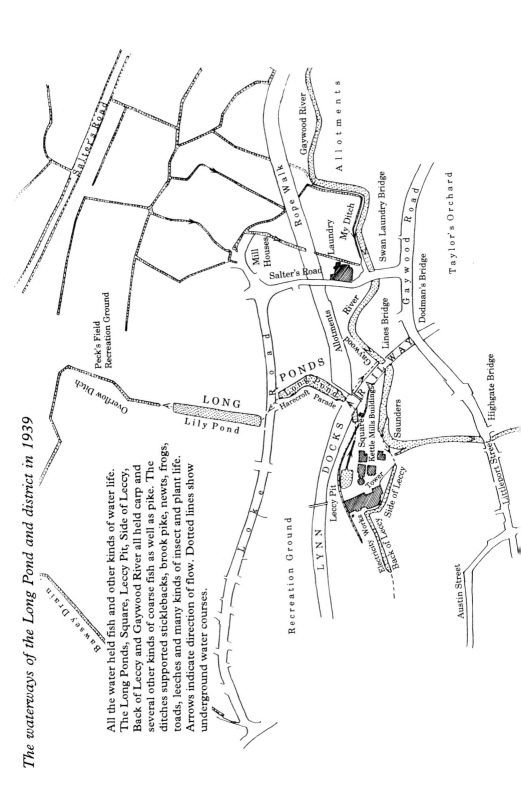

All the water held fish and other kinds of water life. The Long Ponds, Square, Leccy Pit, Side of Leccy, Back of Leccy and Gaywood River all held carp and several other kinds of coarse fish as well as pike. The ditches supported sticklebacks, brook pike, newts, frogs, toads, leeches and many kinds of insect and plant life. Arrows indicate direction of flow. Dotted lines show underground water courses.

Salter's Road

Gaywood River

Allotments

Rope Walk

My Ditch

Laundry

Swan Laundry Bridge

Taylor's Orchard

Mill Houses

Salter's Road

Gaywood Road

Peck's Field Recreation Ground

River

Gaywood

Lines Bridge

Dodman's Bridge

Overflow Ditch

LONG

PONDS

Long Pond

Allotments

R A I L W A Y

Lily Pond

Harecroft Parade

Highgate Bridge

R o a d

DOCKS

Square

Kettle Mills Buildings

Saunders

L o k e

LYNN

Leccy Pit

Tower

Side of Leccy

Littleport Street

Bawsey Drain

Recreation Ground

Electricity Works

Back of Leccy

Austin Street

New World

'Look, Joan! Your bruvver's fishing wivout an 'ook!'

Joan was my elder sister. The speaker was Dowgie, a boy in her class. We had been evacuated only a few days before - on 1st September 1939. A dozen of us were clambering over a small, two-track railway bridge spanning a 25-foot-wide river. The lines themselves were only inches above the water surface. There was a strongish current - partly the river's flow, partly from water gushing out of an enormous pipe, almost entirely submerged, in the left bank as we looked upstream. Bubbles and whirling eddies disappeared under the bridge beneath us, reappeared on the other side, then moved off downstream out of sight round a bend.

The water was silvery green, and its fresh smell was completely new to me. Shoals of small fish swam in shallow water near the banks, and larger ones broke the surface out in the middle. Children wielding nets or cane rods were catching fish nearly all the time.

We had no idea where the railway came from or went to. Fifty yards away in one direction pedestrians, cyclists, horse-drawn vehicles, cars and lorries were crossing over the railway by an iron bridge. The same distance away in the other direction people walked over the railway lines between wide kissing-gates on each side. Around us were orchards, allotments, hedges, back gardens, railway banks and houses. Downstream, on the left, a concrete footpath ran between back yards and the river. But in spite of all the people, movement and noise, it felt overwhelmingly rural and, for us, could hardly have been more different from London.

Those fishing with canes had string tied to the ends, fat floats and bent

1

pins. But Dowgie had somehow acquired a real hook to gut. Having just lost this expensive item in an overhanging apple tree, he threw down the cane, took off his shoes and socks, tucked his short trousers further up, and went paddling with several others. As soon as he was in the water I grabbed his cane, went to the downstream side of the bridge, and began 'fishin' wivout an 'ook'.

The water was so green you could see the bottom only at the sides, so you didn't know what monster fish might be lurking below your float. It was all so mysterious and exciting. Just to hold a piece of fishing equipment was an adventure. To drop the line into a river and see it carried off was magic. Why was a hook necessary? For me, a rod, line and float were enough.

For the rest of the afternoon I happily let the float drift away as far as it could, pulled in, and let it go out again. I expected to catch a fish at any moment, but the fact that I didn't was no disappointment at all.

A war had started. I was evacuated with strange people, in a strange house, in a strange place. But it wasn't because of these things that everything had changed. I already knew that life would never be the same because of fish and fishing.

September 1st, 1939

Leaving London, getting to know new people and places, and having such new experiences had all happened so quickly. Was it really only a few days ago that we had got up early and walked to my sister's school carrying a few sandwiches, a change of clothes and a gas mask? Some parents had brought their children along to be evacuated, changed their minds and taken them home again. But my mother was determined that my sister and I should go, and go together. Nobody in authority knew who was being evacuated and who was not, and we were waiting at the school entrance for some time as names were crossed off or added to lists. Finally we were each given two large labels with a four-figure number on them. I put one round my neck and tied the other to a case. We all lined up and set off westwards towards the City.

At that point my mother, up to then calm and full of advice, burst into tears. It was only the second time I had seen her cry. The first was about seven years earlier when I was four. My father had died and, on the day of the funeral, everyone was crying except me. They all said it was because I didn't understand; but I understood very well, and knew I would never see him again. I wondered now if my mother was crying because she thought she might never see us again. Suppose she was right!

A lot of mothers were in tears by this time, and a friend of my sister's said: 'My Mum's always shouting at me and telling me off, and now she's crying!'

I didn't know the people shepherding us along. Some wore armbands with LCC marked on them. Some had hand luggage, others carried only a gas mask. They kept urging us to keep to the pavements, while they walked in the road or gutter and jumped among us when horses and carts, cars or lorries went by. People stood watching us from doorways and, at first, some waved and called out to the children they knew. But this stopped when we got out of our immediate area. We were soon walking along streets that were only slightly familiar - some of which I would never have dared venture into normally. After about a mile we reached a wider thoroughfare near the City, and could see other queues of children in front and behind, and by the time we reached Liverpool Street Station we were all one, long queue. We shuffled forward into the station where I only just resisted the temptation to slip away into the crowds and run home. We surged forward and were suddenly on a platform, piling into a train which filled up in a few minutes; the doors were slammed and we drew slowly away. A lot of parents came running on to the platform, waving us off. They must have been following us.

The first part of our journey was through familiar territory: half a mile of dark, below-street-level track, and on to Bethnal Green Station where the railway came out above street level. We passed dark, depressing buildings on our left, turned sharply northwards, and were looking down on to Cambridge Heath Road. People below seemed to know we were being evacuated, and waved up at us. We waved back, shouting through the open windows. We went past Bethnal Green Gardens where the library was. There were children playing on the hard surface and by the pond. Bethnal Green Gardens was its official name, but we called it Barmy Park because there had been an asylum there in the past.

We glided past St John's Church, nearly level with the base of its tower. Then came Museum Gardens where I could see the memorial fountain commemorating the bravery of two local people: Alice Maud Denman and Peter Regelous - a great-uncle of ours. They had lost their lives trying to save others in a fire in 1902.

Now the big moment was coming! My mother worked at the Bethnal Green Town Hall, and had arranged to wave to us from there if, when leaving Bethnal Green Station, we turned northwards. We had, and now the Town Hall was only a couple of hundred yards away. Even before we drew level I could see scores of people waving. They waved from the entrance steps and along the pavement in front. They waved from all the windows facing us, and from most of those at the sides. Above the entrance, and below the tower, was a recessed balcony with windows and a statue of a full-size, female, seated figure. The recess was also crowded with people, some of them standing or sitting on the figure itself. Everyone was waving. I waved back, furiously, searching for my mother. We were past, and I was still looking back, waving, when my sister rushed up.

'Did you see Mummy?'

I said I had, but in fact I hadn't recognised her among the scores of people waving. But I was sure my eyes had fallen on everyone there, so I must have seen her. There wasn't time for further discussion because we both rushed to a window on the other side to catch a glimpse of the top floor of a council estate where we lived and from where, so often, we had watched trains just like the one we were in now, billowing smoke on their way out of London. But we were too late, and well past.

For a mile or two we watched other familiar parts of London go slowly by. Then the train picked up speed and, by the time we were going through places we didn't know, everything was flashing past. It was as if the engine driver had purposely been giving us the chance to say goodbye to the places we knew.

London seemed to end suddenly. One moment we were passing back gardens and rows of steel-sided workshops with asymmetrical roofs, the next we were in open countryside. We suddenly felt the need to eat and, very soon, most of my sandwiches were gone.

There were a few stops, but none of them long. A main topic of conversation was where we were going. There were several guesses. The only

Rochelle Street School walking through St James' Park after leaving the station
My teacher and the one who took us to the Point (names alas forgotten) stand on the right. The female teacher on the left is probably Miss Isles the headmistress. Mr Taylor (in spectacles) stands top left. The boy towards the back with open-necked shirt was called Finkelstein. To the right of him and behind are Laurence Berg and his sister.

4

one I remember was Swanage which was, as we later discovered, in almost exactly the opposite direction.

I thought we must have been going for at least six hours when the train came gradually to a stop and there was a lot of shouting. The doors were opened and we were immediately being hustled on to a platform. I happened to be in the front carriage with all my belongings, and as soon as I struggled through the door a man loomed up in front of me.

'Right! Boys! Line up here!'

We were only feet from the ticket barrier. Two bigger boys pushed in front, and I recognised them as the Knottley brothers, one of whom had been at my junior school. A boy I didn't know appeared at my side, and we were already moving away, past the engine, through the barrier and out of the station. We had left Liverpool Street Station just before ten o'clock, and I could see by this station clock it was just after half past twelve. As we went down steps into a wide station yard we were greeted by a loud cheer from crowds of people lining the yard and the street opposite.

We were the first group out, and I never knew if all the following groups were welcomed in the same way. We walked quickly through the crowd and turned right. I glanced behind to see there were about fifteen of us, all boys. I had no idea what had happened to my sister.

Within minutes we were ushered through a door of St James' Girls' Junior School where we filed along, each of us being given a bag of biscuits, a tin of corned beef, a tin of milk and a bar of chocolate. We were out of another door almost immediately and, as we lined up in the same order as before, a man told us we were going to Loke Road: 'One of the longest roads here.'

Mansford Street Central arriving at St James' Girls School, 1st September 1939
The headmaster, Mr Roberts, is on the right wearing a trilby

5

I was to know later that on leaving the school we went via Wyatt Street to the Gaywood Road, and over Dodman's Bridge. As we crossed Gaywood Road a coal lorry came up behind us turning left into Homelands Road. On the running board stood a boy of about ten or eleven holding the cabin door with one hand and a lighted cigarette in the other. As he puffed out smoke a boy behind me shouted:

'Cor! Bli'! What sort of a place have we come to?'

We turned left, and found ourselves in a cul-de-sac at the end of which the houses and pavement went in a tight circle. We had walked two-thirds of the way round this circular part when the man in front stopped and looked up at a first-floor window where a lady's face had just appeared. The man pointed to the two brothers in front.

'Will you take these?'

The lady looked doubtful. 'They're rather big. I'll take the two smaller ones behind.'*

There was no further bargaining. The boy next to me and I went through the gate. I happened to be the first up the stairs and, as the lady opened the door, I went in. I have often thought I might have been the first evacuee billeted in Lynn.

We found ourselves in a bright room. It was only small, but there was a lot of furniture. On our right was a large sideboard. In the middle was a table with chairs round it. There was a mantlepiece over a black fireplace and, in a recess, an enormous wireless set was perched on a small stand. Beside this stood an old, worn armchair with a low seat and a high back. Squashed between the table and a far wall was a kind of settee that I later learnt was a chaise-longue. With the exception of the old armchair all the furniture, door-handles, brass window fittings and even the black fireplace gleamed. Two ladies got up from the chairs and began saying goodbye. The lady of the house invited us to put our things in a bedroom. When we came out, the visitors had gone.

The lady plied us with cups of tea, and we offered her the biscuits and tins of food we had been given. We gave only monosyllabic answers to all her questions and eventually she went off into the kitchen. The other boy and I were left alone, but hardly talked, and I spent most of the time looking out of the window. The houses around the cul-de-sac looked new. In front were tidy gardens and a clean pavement. Beyond the open end of the cul-de-sac a wide road with brick houses and small front gardens receded into the distance. People were walking and cycling there all the time. Suddenly I saw two girls walking along and recognised one as my sister. I yelled 'Joan!', rushed towards the door, and was opening it when the lady came to see what the noise was

*For more information on how evacuees were chosen or allocated, and more general and organisational aspects of evacuation, see *I'll Take That One, Dispelling the Myths of Civilian Evacuation 1939-45'* by Martin Parsons (Beckett Karlson Ltd 1998).

about. I explained:

'It's my kid!'

She smiled. I ran downstairs, through the garden gate and along the pavement. My sister and her friend, having heard the shout, were walking towards me. Joan looked along the cul-de-sac.

'Is that where you're billeted?' Then, seeing my fellow evacuee running up, she said: 'Hello, Henry! Are you billeted with my brother? Hard luck you!'

That was how I learnt the name of the other boy, and that he was at my sister's school.

'Where are you?' I asked.

My sister pointed back along the wide road. 'Along there somewhere. About half a mile.'

The four of us wandered about for some time, meeting and talking to other evacuees, and it was much later in the afternoon that Henry and I returned. We were soon looking out of that first floor window again because the view was so interesting. We were still there when a man on a bicycle turned into the cul-de-sac. He wore overalls and a cap, and had a carrier on the front of his bike. He freewheeled up, leant his bike against the fence in front, came through the gate and entered the doorway below. Hearing footsteps on the stairs, the lady said:

'That sounds like my husband.'

Henry and I immediately found something to do in our bedroom, but it wasn't long before the lady came in.

'Are you coming out? The tea's ready.'

As we sat down at the table the man appeared from another room carrying a mat. He walked round the table, put the mat down on the floor, moved the old armchair from near the window up to the table, and sat down. He was a tallish man but, because he was sitting in an armchair, his face was only just above table height. He smiled up at us. The lady said:

'Well, this is my husband, Mr Peckover, and I'm Mrs Peckover. Come on! Tell us what your names are!' Introduced, we all began to eat.

That evening Henry and I decided to write letters home. When we asked Mrs Peckover for the address, she said it was number twenty-three, Mill Houses, Salter's Road, Loke Road, King's Lynn, Norfolk. Henry and I looked at each other blankly. I did know something about the county of Norfolk. But as for King's Lynn, neither of us had ever heard of the place.

Mill Houses

Early Days

As Henry and I were sitting down for our first breakfast we were surprised to see Mr Peckover appear not from the kitchen or bedroom, but from the front door. He was already wearing boots, overalls and a cap. He nodded and smiled to us as he went through to the kitchen, and we heard sounds of washing from the sink there.

Mrs Peckover must have seen our puzzled looks because she explained: 'Mr Peckover has to go to work very early, then comes home for breakfast.'

'Why does he have to go out so early?' asked Henry.

At that moment Mr Peckover came into the room. He was carrying the mat which he again placed on the floor. Again he moved the old armchair up to the table and sat down. Mrs Peckover said:

'Because he works with horses. Has done all his life, haven't you, Wilfred?'

'That I have,' replied Mr Peckover from his low position.

It was a large breakfast of cereals, eggs, sausages, tomatoes and toast, but Mr Peckover was soon getting up. He moved the armchair back to the window, picked up his mat and disappeared into the kitchen. He was soon back, wearing his cap. He walked to the front door, kissed his wife, said goodbye to us, and went downstairs. From the window we all watched as he got on to his bike. He waved as he went along the cul-de-sac, and again just before going out of sight round the bend.

'He'll be back at ten past twelve,' said Mrs Peckover.

'Do you get up early as well?' I asked.

'Not as early as Mr Peckover, except on a Monday when I get up at four o'clock to do the washing. But I always get up in time to do the housework before breakfast.'

We could see that Mrs Peckover did the housework thoroughly. The flat was spotless. Lino, furniture, windows, brass, ornaments and doors had been polished that morning. Even the fireplace had recently been blacked and polished. On the mantelpiece were two brass cannons about six inches long. They shone with everything else. I exclaimed:

'Crumbs! What are they?'

Mrs Peckover explained: 'They're made from cartridges used in the First World War. Mr Peckover was in that.'

Henry and I stared, wanting to touch them but not daring to. About two years after the outbreak of war a friend of mine was invited into the house, and he took a cannon down to examine it. Mr Peckover said sharply:

'Do you put that back!'

The flat consisted of a living room, kitchen and two bedrooms. But there was a large, walk-in larder with shelves all round from floor to ceiling. Next to that was another space of the same size with, just inside the door, boards across to a height of three feet. This was used for storing coal. Opposite, in a short passage, was a combined bathroom and lavatory. The rooms were small, and there was not much space for four people but, perhaps because everywhere was so tidy, we didn't feel crowded.

Henry was brave enough to ask why Mr Peckover brought in a mat at meal-times.

'It's because of his work,' replied Mrs Peckover. 'He can't help getting his boots mucky because of the horses. And he always has straw, hay and seeds in his clothes.'

Soon after this explanation Mrs Peckover appeared with a brush and dustpan, and carefully swept Mr Peckover's armchair, then the floor where he sat for his meals. Then she fetched a broom and swept a length of lino about two feet wide that was laid over other lino between the kitchen and front doors.

'This is where Mr Peckover has to walk to get in and out in his boots,' she added. To me, that strip of lino looked as new and highly polished as the rest of the floor.

It was not long before Henry and I noticed that behind the house were gardens and open countryside, so we asked if we could explore there. Mrs Peckover said:

'Yes, but you must promise not to touch anything. Don't go into Mr Mindham's garden - our gate is the one in front when you've gone round the corner of the house. You step over a fence at the end of the garden to get to our allotment. And don't fall in the dyke!'

The garden was crowded with flowers and vegetables, and there was an interesting-looking shed with a large padlock. We scrambled over the fence into the allotment, went round a large shed-cum-greenhouse and stared down.

The 'dyke' showing the tunnel under Thurston's field and machine-gun post and Raby Avenue in background

'Water!' I exclaimed.

'What she meant by "dyke" I suppose,' said Henry.

It was a stream about ten feet wide. It came winding across a field opposite, through a tunnel, flowed along the whole length of the allotment, then divided into two. The main part turned at the corner of the allotment, then went off through some trees. We explored, fascinated by the moving water, the weeds, beetles, flies and several shoals of tiddlers. When I suggested

9

trying to jump across, to get to the fields, Henry said:

'What about looking at the pump first?'

'Pump?'

'Didn't you see it? By the greenhouse.'

It was a hand pump, between greenhouse and dyke. From it, neat steps were cut down the bank to the water. As I examined the steps, Henry shouted:

'A copper!'

It was enormous, about three feet deep, as much across and half full with bright green water. I got hold of the pump handle and pushed backwards and forwards, tentatively.

'She said we shouldn't touch anything,' warned Henry.

'I wonder if it works,' I said.

After a few more strokes I felt the handle stiffen, and a dribble of water came out into the copper. I kept on pumping, and water gushed out strongly to the accompaniment of loud thumping noises from somewhere below ground. Henry watched for a short time, claimed it was his turn, and began pumping furiously. The whole apparatus thumped even more loudly, and trembled violently. The copper filled up, and water began overflowing down the bank. Suddenly the water stopped, and Henry was working a very loose handle. I said:

'You did it!'

That evening, when we were eating, Mr Peckover looked up from his low position.

'Some great lummox has been a-fillin' up th'old copper and jiggered the pump!'

Mrs Peckover frowned at us. 'You are naughty boys!' She looked down at her husband. 'I told them not to touch anything.'

'That's all right,' he said. 'That there washer always come off if you go a-pumpin' too hard. I've put it back on.' Fortunately that was the end of the matter.

Mr Peckover must have always done a lot of work, and been hungry by midday, and that was when they had their main meal. On the third day, promptly at ten minutes past twelve, Mrs Peckover served up a large piece of pudding with gravy. Henry and I waited for something else to be put with it but, when both our hosts began eating, we exchanged glances and began eating ourselves. When Henry had finished he put down his knife and fork and said:

'When *we* have this at home, we have other things with it. We eat more than you do.'

'That you don't,' said Mr Peckover.

Mrs Peckover said: 'That'd puzzle me!' She went to the kitchen, and returned with several saucepans of meat and vegetables. That was our first experience of eating Yorkshire pudding before the rest.

Although school did not start up immediately, we reported to a school building several times a week. Each time we were given large, brown paper bags full of biscuits. At first we gorged ourselves, but soon grew sick of them. We gave large quantities to our hosts who then began giving them to neighbours and anyone else who would take them. Soon, hardly anyone could face another biscuit. One day some of us were returning to our billets having again been loaded with biscuits. Reaching St James' Park we tied our bags at the neck and began throwing them up into trees. Some bags lodged up, out of sight, but others came down and broke open. By the time we ran off, hundreds of biscuits were lying about beneath the trees, and paper bags were blowing everywhere. Some people stopped to watch us. They probably thought we were a wasteful, rough and ungrateful lot of Londoners.

We hadn't been evacuated a week, and were having breakfast one morning when the sound of breaking glass and crunching wood came from outside. We all rushed to the window. Just below was the milkman's cart. It was horse-drawn, but the horse was rearing up and pushing backwards. The cart was at a crazy angle, sending bottles crashing on to the road. Old Ted Mindham from the flat below rushed through the gate and began reaching up to the reins. Mr Peckover ran downstairs. Ted Mindham seemed to enrage the horse even more, and nearly disappeared under the animal. Mr Peckover arrived and reached up to the harness. The horse stopped rearing and immediately calmed down. Mr Peckover began talking to it and stroking its neck, and led it forward so the cart righted itself. It was only then that the milkman came running up. There was a brief conversation between the three men, and Mr Peckover came upstairs and finished his breakfast. He explained to Mrs Peckover what had been wrong, but all I understood was that something was too tight. Mr Peckover must have seen what was wrong immediately, and had acted quickly.

The second Sunday morning after breakfast, Henry and I lost no time in getting down to the dyke. We were soon wet and plastered with mud, so decided to go away for a while and dry off. Henry was finishing off some frantic pumping. I had just come up the steps, and saw a small boy standing behind Henry. I must have looked surprised because Henry turned round. He stopped pumping and demanded:

'Who are you?'

The boy, only about six years old, simply stared, not replying. Henry picked up a plank of wood, raised it above his head, and went up to the boy.

'Who are you?'

The boy looked too frightened to reply, and Henry made as if to bring the plank down on his head.

I didn't think Henry would really hit the boy. Such threatening behaviour was fairly normal to us at the time. But I grabbed the plank from Henry's hands and held it behind my back. He didn't resist or even protest. The boy still seemed too afraid to talk, or even run away, so I led him off to the house. He was Jack, a nephew of Mr and Mrs Peckover's, and often came to visit them on a Sunday morning with his mother. He continued to come all through the war, and we have been friends ever since. But we didn't speak about that incident until nearly sixty years later

The Long Pond

The Long Pond was in two parts. The half I got to know first was a hundred and twenty yards long, twenty yards wide, and only two hundred yards from Mill Houses. Its banks were lined with anglers from four years of age upwards. Each had a cane with line tied to the end, and a float of cork and trimmed feather. Bait was usually bread or flour paste, and most hooks were a bent pin. There was a constant hubbub as anglers talked of bites, baits and fish. Claims of 'Garim!' rang out as small, struggling fish were hauled clear of the water. Those not getting bites tended to move where fish had just been caught so that, in places, young anglers were not only side by side, but also fishing from higher up the bank over others' heads. There were frequent shouts as lines became entangled and the owners tried to separate them, impatient to start fishing again.

Water was pumped through the Long Pond from the nearby electricity generating station, so it was always warm, often hot, and vapour rose from it. This vapour was especially dense in the mornings and, in cold weather, it was sometimes impossible to see a float out in the middle. When it was getting dark, anglers sometimes used a torch to get a sight of their float. The vapour, responding to the slightest movements of air, formed a never-ending kaleidoscope of fantastic patterns just above the surface.

This part of the pond was shaped like a cricket bat with a very short handle and the blade broken in the middle to an angle of forty-five degrees. Water came in from the generating station through a six-foot-wide tunnel under the railway, and this width was continued for seven yards by concrete banks with vertical sides a foot above water level. This was the short handle. In one of the concrete sides was a three-foot diameter pipe with bars across where water flowed away strongly into the Gaywood River at the railway bridge.

The concrete sides were about four feet wide, so where they ended abruptly the pond became that much wider on both sides. From here, grassy banks curved away sharply to form the pond's full width. This is where the cricket bat blade started.

From both sides, where concrete and grass bank met, bits of wooden fencing jutted out at an angle into the water. Although only a few feet long, each fence often supported four or five young anglers, their lines out in different directions. The post tops, hollowed by weathering, held lumps of bait and other belongings.

From this end the pond stretched for sixty yards. Then it turned left at forty-five degrees and went on for another sixty yards - this part being the bottom half of the cricket bat's broken blade. The pond ended a few yards from the Loke Road pavement.

Along both sides of the pond, about two-thirds of the way from Loke Road to the railway, were houses. Between their front gardens and the pond's banks were narrow access roads where, just behind the young anglers, deliveries of coal, milk, bread, meat and groceries took place much of the time.

Map of Lynn adapted from the Ordnance Survey of 1928

On one side, the access road narrowed to a footpath where people walked and cycled. They chatted as they manœuvred their bikes through the kissing-gates on each side of the railway, or stood about having conversations that carried clearly across the water. The men were usually on their way to or from work, or their allotments; the women to or from shopping. Errand boys on delivery bikes swept swiftly between pedestrians and other cyclists, sometimes stopping to talk to friends or watch fish being caught.

13

At the end of the houses on the other side of the pond the access road was blocked by a high, wire-netting fence negotiable by only the most agile. So pedestrians and cyclists didn't go along here, and it was on these grassy banks that children played games that were at first incomprehensible to me.

People living in the surrounding houses were often talking at their gates, gardening, sweeping the pavement in front, or shouting to neighbours across the pond. So close were some of the houses to the water that it looked possible to fish from their first-floor windows.

From the Loke Road end of the pond came noises of horse-drawn vehicles, tractors, lorries, cars and motor-bikes. From the other end came train hoots and whistles, and the noise of long lines of trucks clattering in both directions along the railway. People waited, then rushed across the lines as soon as one lot of trucks had passed, and before the next came along.

Near the kissing-gates the two-track railway widened into three, and it was here that shunting went on, with puffing of engines, stuttering of trucks, and shouts of railwaymen wielding shunting poles.

Just the other side of the railway was the electricity generating station, so to all the other noises were added hisses of steam, whistles and a siren which was already the town's air raid warning. In damp weather even the pylon at the railway end emitted a loud crackling noise.

Sometimes there were as many dogs as anglers. Some ran about, barking. Others sat or lay on the grass. Yet others walked past giving the impression that they, like the people walking or cycling, had a definite destination in mind - which I later discovered many of them had.

Yet in spite of all the people, dogs, movement and noise, there was a feeling of space. Houses didn't have other buildings looming behind them, so you could see sky between them and above their roofs. Nearby allotments added to the feeling of openness, and so did the swathe of railway which was separated from houses, allotments and orchards by trees, high hedges and green embankments. The horizon beyond the railway was mainly trees, with only a few roofs visible. It was all very different from London.

Along both sides of the pond, about two-thirds of the way from Loke smallest cracks in pavements and roads. Reeds grew in the shallower water. Birds flew low over the water, some of them touching it. Others landed on the grass to take bits of bread bait that anglers threw to them. There were clouds of flies over water and banks; bees hummed and wasps zoomed. Even on the hottest days there was a fresh breeze blowing.

This wasn't all! Just the other side of Loke Road was the other half of the Long Pond: dead straight, about the same width and slightly longer. Although part of the Long Pond it was called the Lily Pond because of the lilies that grew thickly almost all over it. Water from the other side flowed into it under the road, and there was a continuous current where it poured out. The water over this side was distinctly cooler with seldom any vapour rising. The Lily

The Railway end of the Long Pond

Pond, too, had paths and access roads all round it, but it was less hemmed in by houses, and many of these were sideways on. At the far end was a drain where water flowed away. There were fewer anglers here than over the other side, probably because of the difficulty of fishing among the lilies. In the shallow water at the Loke Road end shoals of fish, some of them a foot long, swam inches from the side.

I longed to be one of those young anglers catching fish and talking about them. Could that ever happen? Would I ever have a cane rod? And if I did, would I ever dare to come and fish among all these knowledgeable anglers?

The Key

One Sunday morning Mr Peckover asked Henry and me if we'd like a walk. Henry, suspicious, asked:

'How far is it?'

'A mile or two,' replied Mr Peckover.

'I think I'll stay around here,' said Henry.

I decided to go. As we walked across the Tuesday Market Place Mr Peckover told me he was visiting his parents and would take me an interesting way round. I had heard my hosts talking about Mr Peckover's parents, and had the impression that the father was a very hard sort of man.

Mr Peckover said:'Course, I bike there as a rule. They live in South Lynn, but I thought you might want to see a bit of Lynn.'

We saw wharves, ships and a railway along the banks of the River Ouse before coming out on to a main road. It had been an exciting walk and, with my running about exploring, I covered twice the distance Mr Peckover had. As we came to a main road, Mr Peckover said:

'This is it, Saddlebow Road.' We walked for a while before turning into a house numbered eighty-one, on our left.

Mr Peckover told his mother who I was, then shouted a simplified version at enormous volume into his father's ear. Turning to me he explained that you had to shout because his father was deaf. He said it in a voice I was sure his father must have heard. Mr Peckover senior didn't look a hard man at all. He smiled all the time, and soon took me into a different room, and pointed to a photograph hanging on the wall. It was of some kind of machine.

'That's where I used to work,' he said, proudly.

I asked him what kind of machine it was, but he merely nodded and smiled.

Mrs Peckover senior told me all about her family. Her daughter, Ethel, had been to the Girls' High School. Her other son, Cyril, was unmarried, and still lived with them. He was interested in only one thing, railways. He had worked on them since he left school. He chatted to me about railways, and what it was like to be an engine driver. Then he said:

'You must be tired, Ken, walking all that way, and running around. Would you like to lie down for a bit?'

Mrs Peckover senior showed me into the room with the photo, and I lay down on a settee. After a minute or two I noticed a man's jacket hanging from a hook just above, one of its pockets invitingly open by my head. I patted the pocket and it made a jingling noise. There was something metallic in it. I put a hand into the pocket, felt around, and pulled out two pennies and an enormous key. It looked very old, and I wondered what it could be for. I admired it for a while, then put it into my own pocket, together with the two pennies. A few minutes later I took out the coins and returned them to the jacket pocket. Some time later, when I heard someone coming, I returned the key also. It felt exciting having such a key in my own pocket, and I would have liked to know what it was for. I didn't ask.

We went home a much shorter way, but it was long enough for me to realise I was glad the coppers and key weren't still in my pocket. It was such a wonderful key. Heavy, big and complicated. Even the handle part had more to it than ordinary keys. What kind of door would it have fitted? I never found out.

Sandbagging

'Seen what they're doing on the rec., Reg?'

It was the elder of the two Kendall brothers who lived near the other end of the Loke. I had got to know them on the recreation ground, and couldn't imagine what was happening apart from the usual playing on slide, swings and roundabout with, perhaps, arrows being shot high into the air.

'They're getting on with that A.R.P. place, and some boys are helping!'

I sprinted a hundred yards along to see the far corner of the rec., by the Loke, a hive of activity. I had already seen that the skeleton of a building had been put up, but now a large heap of sand lay beside it. Men were standing all over the framework, and a group of boys, with one or two girls, were busily filling sandbags - some of which had already been laid at ground level.

I ran up to the nearest man. 'Can I help?'

The man pointed to a boy who was trying to hold a bag and fill it up at the same time. 'Join up with him! You're just in time; that's the last shovel.'

Lynn children helping to fill sandbags on the Loke Road recreation ground
Lynn News & Advertiser, September 5th 1940

The other boy and I took it in turns to shovel sand and hold bags. We worked frenetically, and I wondered how long I could keep up the pace. I wasn't the last one, and several more boys arrived, filling up bags with their hands. We kept the men busy, putting the bags on sides and top of the A.R.P. post, and they kept rejecting bags because they had either too little or too much sand in them. Eventually one man had the job of looking at our bags before they were tied up, to make sure they were correctly filled. By this time even more children had arrived and were dragging sandbags along to where they were needed.

I got back to Mill Houses late for the meal, and with sand in socks and shoes, down my back and in my hair. Mrs Peckover had been worried, and now wasn't very pleased. She put down some newspapers for me to change on, but when she heard what important work we'd been doing she didn't seem to mind too much. By the time I had left, the A.R.P. post was covered with sandbags and the men were going home.

My Ditch

'That's a net!' exclaimed Mr Peckover. He must have mistaken my look of incredulity for puzzlement.

'I know what it is!' I said. 'It's a proper fishing net.' It consisted of a wooden handle about four feet long, a stout loop of wire and part of an old stocking.

'That's for both on yer,' warned Mr Peckover, waving the net towards Henry and me.

Mrs Peckover added: 'And if there are any arguments about it, he'll take it back.'

'That I will,' confirmed Mr Peckover. 'And I'll chop it up too!'

Henry wasn't very interested, and used it only once. He didn't mind when I began taking it everywhere with me.

The net wasn't much use in the deeper waters of the Long Pond, the Square or some of the Gaywood River, and would have disturbed the proper anglers there. But this didn't matter because there were ditches, dykes and streams everywhere, all teeming with water life. Using the net I soon discovered that even places looking like temporary flood-water or large puddles often supported all kinds of weeds, insects and even sticklebacks.

One favourite place was a ditch only about two minutes' walk from home. I didn't realise at first that it was fed by the dyke at the end of Mr Peckover's allotment. It ran for two hundred yards between Green's garage and the Swan Laundry bridge, parallel to the Gaywood River and only about ten feet from it. In places it was nearly two feet deep; in others only about six inches. Some parts dried up in summer. It had probably served as an overflow for the river itself. There were sedges, reeds and lots of aquatic plants, and it abounded with creatures I had never seen before, but which I learnt were various kinds of larvæ, whirligigs, water-boatmen, water spiders and several kinds of crustacea. But there were also things I recognised from the start, like newts, frogs, sticklebacks and, in spring, frogspawn and tadpoles. In winter, when it was frozen over, you could still see sticklebacks darting about below the ice.

I called the place 'My Ditch'.

At first I used to scoop about indiscriminately with the net, excited about what I might catch. Later on I used it more carefully, not wanting to disturb the creatures there. So I spent a lot of time just looking down into the water to see what was happening. For such a small ditch there was so much life! How did it all get there? How did it manage to survive from year to year?

One day I noticed a stickleback in shallow water. It didn't look very well and I fished it out carefully with the net. A leech was attached to its side. I held them under water for a few minutes wondering what to do. Should I leave the leech, and let nature take its course? Were leeches bad? They must play some part in nature.

18

In the end I removed the leech and put it back in the same place, then put the stickleback some yards away in deeper water. It swam off strongly, and hadn't looked damaged, so I convinced myself I'd done the right thing.

Lynn abounded with ditches and other bits of clean water, all full of life. They were all beautiful, but I had a special feeling for 'My Ditch' and spent a lot of time there, never going over the Swan Laundry bridge without having a look.

What's in a Name?

It was a simple matter for Mr and Mrs Peckover to call us 'Henry' and 'Ken', but what were we to call them? When talking to other people we could refer to them as 'Mr and Mrs Peckover' or as 'hosts' or, more often, 'lady' or 'man':

'What's your lady like?'

'What does your man do?'

'Do your man and lady give you pocket money?'

But how could we address them on a day-to-day basis? For us it was too much of a mouthful, and too embarrassing, to keep saying 'Mr Peckover' or 'Mrs Peckover' all the time, and not many evacuees went that way about it. Some, either because they were invited to, or because it came naturally, used 'Aunt' or 'Uncle'. Some went as far as to use first names also:

'What time shall I get back, Aunty Margaret?'

'Uncle John, could I borrow your penknife, please?' (One wartime evacuee, now seventy years old, still refers to his hosts as 'Uncle Ted' and 'Aunty Kate'.)

I never dared use 'Uncle' or 'Aunt'. For one thing, I was never asked to. For another, it seemed a presumption about being as closely related as our hosts' niece and nephew were.

Our hosts also had the advantage of being able to use their own name, or relationships. He could say: 'Leave Mrs Peckover's bike outside the shed. She's using it this afternoon.' She could say: 'I don't think my husband's going to be back very early this evening.'

One London friend, billeted in Smith Avenue, had an unusual solution to the problem. His host was a widower with several grown-up sons and daughters living with him. His name was Mr Knights, and the evacuee called him, simply, 'Knights'.

'Hello, Knights, like me to take the dog for a walk?' or 'When's the meal going to be ready, Knights?'

This seemed an appropriate arrangement for them because their relationship consisted mainly of jokey backchat. Or perhaps that arrangement gave rise to the relationship.

That evacuee called all the grown-up sons and daughters by their first names too. I have often wondered what my friend would have called Mr Knights' wife had she been alive.

I couldn't see Mr Peckover being happy with 'Peckover' though. From the stories he told about what happened at work, I knew his superiors called him that.

Ken Regelous with Mr and Mrs Peckover

For Henry and me it seemed sensible, and not too long-winded, to use 'Mr' when talking to Mrs, and 'Mrs' when talking to Mr:

'Is Mr Peckover in the garden?'

'Mrs Peckover asks if you'd bring up some firewood.'

Perhaps it was because of these awkwardnesses that both Henry and I initiated conversation as seldom as possible, and waited until spoken to. We could then carry on a conversation without using names at all. But if we *had* to start talking, we tried to gain attention first. If I had broken something, for example, I'd go up to Mr Peckover, wave the object in front of him, and ask:

'Look! This broke today. Do you think it's mendable?'

He would then either promise to mend it, or get his tools out straight away, and I hadn't had to use a name at all. It might not always be as quick as that. Once, Henry stood behind Mrs Peckover when she was busy at the sink. When she turned round he held out a sixpence and asked if she had change. But he'd had to wait about ten minutes for her to turn round!

For Mrs Peckover there was never a name problem. She called Henry 'Henry', and me by my full name 'Kenneth'. For Mr Peckover there was no difficulty with the 'Henry', but he had some embarrassment with 'Kenneth'. He always said this at home but, when outside and when Mrs Peckover wasn't there, he seemed to prefer 'Ken'.

Our hosts were also in a position to be jokey. Mr Peckover would often ask me: 'What have you been up to this morning, spondulix?'

Or, referring to Henry, he might ask Mrs Peckover: 'When's his lordship on school this week? Morning or afternoon?'

Referring to me, he might ask: 'Did his highness get a wettin' today?'

When waking us up in the morning, Mrs Peckover would always say: 'Come on! Wake up England!'

So the adults had all the advantages, and we were more affected by the unusual circumstances. Our hosts were neither peers nor relatives. But nor were they strangers. We lived in their house, but had no idea how long we would continue to do so. And it was a relationship that could end without warning. Some of the reasons I heard, in the early days especially, for wanting to get rid of evacuees were:

'There isn't room in the house.'

'My husband doesn't want them any more.'

'They can't get on with my own children.'

'The dog won't take to them.'

'I don't have the time now.'

'They're too messy.'

'They're disobedient.'

'They won't get up in the morning.'

The relationship could also be ended by the evacuee. This was often done by a letter home complaining of something, and the parent would arrive in Lynn either to take the child back to London or to find another billet. Several of my own friends consulted a teacher - who would usually try to patch up misunderstandings or suggest compromises.

One common complaint by evacuees was not being able to sleep properly and always feeling tired. Often this turned out to be the result of both going to bed and getting up earlier than at home. They couldn't get used to it. Another was feeling ill or sick much of the time. This did sometimes seem to be the result of different food. Since it was the unhappy ones who made such specific complaints, it seemed to me at the time that homesickness was at the bottom of a lot of it. When an evacuee was homesick there wasn't a lot even the most welcoming and considerate hosts could do about it. It was often soon after the first change of billet that the evacuee went home, probably having convinced the parents that Lynn wasn't the place for them.

From the very beginning evacuees were returning home in large numbers and, by the beginning of 1940, when the number was at about its maximum in Lynn, the comings and goings meant daily changes to our school register.

The rate of return of the first lot of us must have been very high indeed. I knew a lot of children on the train we arrived in, and never saw some of them again. The Knottley brothers who had been in front of us in the queue at Mill Houses, for example, I have never seen since, yet they must have been billeted that day. So must the rest of the boys in that group, although I only ever saw two of them again. A week or two after we arrived a neighbour in London, who was a coach driver, drove a coachload of parents to Lynn. When it left that evening, it carried back several evacuees with their parents.

21

Winter in the Country

Before the war a friend, Don Nicholson, and I used sometimes to try and walk out of London into 'the country'. The furthest we travelled was the few miles to the Hackney Marshes - a large, open area with a river running through it, and bounded by a canal on one side. Don's elder sister and my own were at the same secondary school when war broke out, and all four of us were evacuated to Lynn together. Here, Don and I could easily satisfy our ambition to walk to the country, and to *real* marshes. We had only to go past Peck's Field, turn right through the allotments and cross the small, iron bridge over Clark's Dyke. But the walk to that iron bridge was itself a country walk to us. We'd start off behind the Raby Avenue houses along a track known as Salter's Road. It was a path between gardens and a dyke - where we saw sticklebacks, newts and frogs. Further along, when we turned off into Raby Avenue itself we saw, as often as not, half a dozen ducks rooting about in front gardens or crossing the road. This was a memorable experience in itself, but more striking was the dog that was usually with them. It went with them everywhere, and when the ducks were in single file the dog was often in line with them too. This unlikely combination was once the subject of an article in a local newspaper.

Only fifty yards the other side of the iron bridge was an embankment that made a sharp turn round a hollow and, because of its shape, we began calling it 'The Cockpit'. Soon, Mr and Mrs Peckover were using the same name. Then some of their friends began using it. Eventually all the Londoners who knew the marshes were using the name, and so were lots of Lynn children.

If we were at school in the morning, Don and I would explore the marshes in the afternoon. If we had afternoon school, we would go to the marshes in the morning. One morning we were late back from the marshes, and late for afternoon school, and after that Don's hosts wouldn't let him go over the marshes in the morning. We explored the marshes right through the winter of 1939-40. I would get out after the midday meal and run to the recreation ground in Loke Road. There I would wait on the swings until Don, who was billeted opposite the rec., came running across the snow.

That winter the snow lay about for weeks and weeks, and the wind formed long drifts all over the marshes. Some drifts were three feet high and we could make large holes through them. At the time we had a craze for whips. Don had seen a Zorro film, and would describe scenes from it which we acted out. I hadn't seen the film, and was very envious. However, Don had only a rudimentary whip, whilst I had a proper one made for me by Mr Peckover. The handle was a piece of ash, with a leather loop. To this I could attach different lashes which also had leather loops. To these, in turn, I could fasten thin end-lengths made of Mr Peckover's snobbing twine, knotted in

The Water Tower from Harecroft Parade in winter, St Nicholas spire in background

places to prevent fraying. With our whips we made a Z, for Zorro, every few yards for miles over the marshes.

Another attraction of the marshes was the large number of shotgun cartridges we found, and my bedroom was soon overflowing with them. One day we found a bundle of clothes floating in a ditch with, beside it, a message about Polish prisoners-of-war. We searched everywhere for a dead body, convinced there was one somewhere near. Mr and Mrs Peckover were both interested in hearing what came of it all. To our disappointment nothing ever did.

We sometimes got to the marshes by going right along Turbus Road to the 'bridge that went nowhere'. This was a stone bridge over Clark's Dyke complete with road, pavements and parapets. It took Turbus Road high over the dyke, but stopped abruptly on the other side where it met grass.

For weeks on end the snow didn't melt, and the frequent snowfalls were cleared from in front of shops and houses, and pushed into high ridges along the roadsides. This made the roads of the town much narrower. It was difficult to walk or cycle without slipping. Cars and lorries had chains fitted to their wheels. Horses often slipped over, and it could be a long job getting them back on to their feet. Mr Peckover then worked a pair of horses at Leake's Mill and had calkins fitted into the horses' shoes. The calkins were made of metal, something over an inch long with a thread at one end and tapered to an edge at the other. He gave me one of these, and it was a treasured possession for many years.

The snow went very slowly, but for a long time the icy ridges remained along roadsides, and it seemed to me they never completely disappeared because small ridges, that hadn't been there before as far as I could remember, remained permanently.

In Mill Houses the small open fire was the only means of heating except for a paraffin stove which we sometimes had in the bathroom. The living room had four doors leading from it so, although the fire was very effective, if a door was left open there were immediate shouts of 'Put the wood in the hole!' In my bedroom was a marble-topped washstand with a bowl of water standing on it, and when I got up in the mornings the water was frozen -even on a Monday when Mrs Peckover did her early morning wash in the kitchen copper making my bedroom wall as hot as a radiator.

Old School Ties

I had high hopes of school once we were evacuated. The London junior school I attended up to the war was all-boys, and dominated by the aim of winning scholarships to local grammar schools or Christ's Hospital. So hardly anything except maths and English was done in the final year. Nor was there a daily dose of both those subjects; it was maths all day, or English all day. For one period in that final year we spent weeks copying maths problems into our exercise books from the blackboard and textbooks. All day and every day was spent on this. Then we spent several more weeks working through them all day. The teacher never helped, nor did we want him to because when we didn't understand something we were shouted at and sent off to get the answer from younger classes. One day we were doing maths, all working quietly, and I was getting along quickly. But I happened to look up, working out something in my head. The teacher immediately shouted at me to come out. I took my book out, my mind a complete blank. I hoped he would see that I had been getting on very well, but he barked out:

'Well, what's a quarter of sixty?'

I was in such a state I didn't even understand the question, or why he'd asked it. I was still trying to think, when he dragged me to the door.

'Go and ask Mr Jones' class what a quarter of sixty is!'

Mr Jones was sympathetic and, instead of bringing his younger pupils into it, quietly looked through my exercise book.

'Some of these are very hard! You've found a quarter of much more difficult numbers, even fractions. How do you normally do it?'

I immediately saw two ways of doing it, and wondered why I hadn't been able to do it before. But when I returned to my own class, and the teacher asked me what the answer was, I almost couldn't answer again.

One day, one of the older boys went out to the teacher's desk carrying three exercise books.

'I've finished them all, sir.'

There was a gasp from the class. Most of us hadn't got anywhere near finishing the questions we had spent weeks copying down. The teacher took the exercise books, flicked through them and looked up at us (the room was tiered).

'That's the standard I expect all of you to reach.' With that, he handed the exercise books back to the boy, who returned to his place.

The only respite we normally had from written maths was a ten-minute session of mental arithmetic but one day, out of the blue, the teacher announced we were going to do geography. With joy we opened our desks and took out the new, unused geography text books. There was half an hour's welcome geography, then we returned to the maths problems.

Perhaps it was the school conditions that explained some of our behaviour. During the play-breaks we would run around, knocking into others and fighting, throwing and kicking balls non-stop and swinging on playground shelter rafters until our arms ached. Sometimes we could let off steam in the classroom as well because the teacher often went out for long periods, leaving us to our own devices.

For much of the school year there was a large, open fire blazing at the front. As soon as the teacher went out, one of us would creep to the door and keep watch, while someone else put the long poker into the fire. As soon as it was red hot someone would run out, take the poker, push it right through the floorboards, and put it back beside the fire. The floor of that classroom had scores of holes burnt through it.

When the teacher returned he would often know there was an extra hole, and there would follow a long inquisition as he tried to find out who did it. I don't think he ever did.

We were less careful if, with the teacher absent, we were not actually burning holes in the floor. The room would be in uproar as we shouted and fought battles. Then, suddenly, the door would be open, and the teacher standing there noting the half-dozen boys furthest from their desks. Then followed canings in an empty room at the very top of the building.

At that time I had only to think about school to feel my stomach turn over, and I know a lot of others felt the same. I once had a day off when an uncle took me to the London Zoo. The next day, explaining my absence, I told the teacher that my uncle had arranged to take me to the zoo, but I hadn't gone because I was sick. I was convinced that anything true must be blameworthy.

For a while, after evacuation, there was no school. When it started up it was only half-time because of the large numbers of evacuees and the shortage of school buildings. For a reason we never understood I was put not into the secondary school, but into a London junior school, Rochelle Street, based in St James' Boys' building. We did mornings only, or afternoons only, on alternate weeks. Morning sessions were the more popular because, although it meant getting up earlier, we were free from midday to do as we liked. Leaving school at midday we would meet those arriving for the afternoon session, and laugh at them. But when we were on the afternoon session, coming to school, we would laugh at those going home for having

LYNN SCHOOLS RE-OPEN

Shift System Adopted for Evacuees

NOVEL EXPERIMENTS IN EDUCATION

THE LYNN ELEMENTARY school's re-opened yesterday (Monday) at 9 a.m. The senior departments are not affected by the arrival of evacuated children from London schools and will continue their work at the usual times.

All the infant and junior departments were open to Lynn children for one extended session only each day. During the present week this will be from 9 a.m. until 1 p.m., and next week from 1 p.m. until 5 p.m., and similarly on mornings and afternoons in alternate weeks. In some cases it may be deemed an advantage to open at 8.45 a.m. and close at 12.45 p.m., in order to provide an interval between the two school sessions.

25

had to get up early, and having spent the morning at school. So, around midday, roads near St James' Boys' school were full of children pointing at each other, jeering, and helpless with laughter.

Although the junior school had been on the same train as we had, they went off in the opposite direction when leaving the station, and were billeted on the other side of town. So I seldom met other pupils outside school during the first term, and knew nobody there. The standard of maths and English was well below what I had been used to and the teachers, far from being pleased about this, seemed to take it as an insult that someone from a different school was further ahead. I was labelled as a rebel by the staff because I refused to put on my gas mask when practices were held. My reason was that every time I put it on, even if only for a few seconds, I got a painful stye which lasted a week or more. Since the practices were held weekly, I would have had a permanent stye. For other reasons, like having to defend myself in the playground, or being unfamiliar with some of the school rules, I was often sent to the headmistress for caning. On one of these occasions she was just bringing the stick down when I withdrew my hand. She claimed to have hit her foot, was furious, and lashed out wildly calling me a coward. When I went home that day I told Mr and Mrs Peckover what had happened, and they both burst out laughing. That made me feel somewhat better.

I wasn't really interested in maths, having been put off at the London school, but now, to be awkward, I wanted to outshine the others - including the teachers - in that subject. Although I was a sport fanatic I pretended to have no interest in games. In the London school I had played in the school team, and was the first one there ever to own a pair of real football boots. One day the Rochelle Street teacher brought in some copies of a book about football. None of the girls wanted one, but all the boys except me were given one - although some of them tried to refuse. There was one copy over, and the teacher took it back to her desk and sat down. She thumbed through it, then looked at me.

'You're not interested in things like football, are you?'

I replied: 'Not in the slightest.' I am sure it was my professed lack of interest that prompted her to say:

'You might as well have it. I don't want to throw it away.'

That book became one of my most prized possessions. There were stories about famous football matches and famous footballers. One chapter was entitled: 'Bastin, the Best Boy of All'. There was a photograph of Bryn Jones, knocking studs into his boots, with a caption explaining that he had gone to Arsenal for a record fee. Another photograph showed that Derby County's winning goal had been scored just after the ball had gone over the goal line. I had never seen such a wonderful book, and soon knew it almost by heart. The teacher could never have guessed what pleasure it gave me.

One teacher was different. He played the violin, and sometimes gave a recital in the school hall. He once played music by Schubert and Schumann, and introduced them by telling us something about their lives and music. His eyes shone with pleasure and excitement as he talked and played. That was the first time I had heard anyone talking in glowing terms about a German and an Austrian.

Pupils from the secondary school next door, including my sister, came along to one of his recitals. When he announced he was going to play 'Who is Sylvia?' there was a buzz of excitement from those older pupils at the back of the hall. The teacher looked up, delighted with the interest, and I decided that this man lived in a different, and nicer, world than the others.

It was a cold, winter's day when my own class joined with another for a visit to the banks of the River Ouse to see how the Dutch settlers once went about preventing erosion of the banks. Mr and Mrs Peckover advised me to wear 'water boots' for the outing. I was of course still in short trousers, and by the time I had walked to school, then to the Point, the tops of my wellingtons had cut my legs, which were sore and bleeding. The two lady teachers noticed this and, quite horrified, examined the sore places. As they went off, one said to the other:

'He must have peculiar skin! I've never seen anything like it before, yet he didn't even complain.'

My own teacher replied: 'Well, boys like that don't feel pain.'

As 1940 wore on it began to look as if I was going to be stuck in that school for good. So, when leaving the building one afternoon, I decided that if I couldn't make a move to the other school officially, I'd do it another way. One day, instead of turning into the Junior School, I would go straight on to the Secondary School only a few yards away.

Canes

It was a school holiday. As I went indoors, after spending all morning exploring with the net, Mrs Peckover greeted me:

'Don't go into the kitchen yet. Mr Peckover's doing something in there.'

'What is it?'

'Well, it's a secret.'

'How long will it be a secret?'

Mrs Peckover laughed. 'Only till Henry gets back. He's gone to give a message to Mrs Fayers in South Clough Lane. It's a surprise for the two of you.'

As soon as Henry came into sight I opened the window.

'Hurry up! There's a surprise for us!'

Henry broke into a run. When he arrived, Mrs Peckover opened the kitchen door slightly.

'Can they come in yet?'

'Ah!'

We pushed through. Mr Peckover was standing there holding two canes about ten feet long. A length of his shoe-repairing twine was hanging from each.

'Rods!' I shouted.

Mr Peckover nodded. 'You'll be able to do some proper fishing now.'

He propped the canes against a wall, went over to the copper, and picked up the army haversack he always took to work. It was open at the top. Slipping a hand inside, he produced a brand new float; it was white, with a blue top. He took off the small rubber ring, threaded it on to one of the lines, pushed the float back, and pulled the free end of the line through the float's bottom eye.

'Right! This is yours, Henry.' From the haversack he drew out another float. It was exactly the same as the first, but with a green top. I immediately decided green was much better than blue.

'This one's yours, Ken.' He fitted it on, and went to the haversack again. As soon as I saw the small, transparent paper packet, I exclaimed:

'Hooks! Proper ones to catgut!'

'That's right.' He tied a hook to each of the lines. Again he went to the haversack and put a hand inside. There was a distinctive rattle, and I knew what it was before he'd got it out.

'Weights!'

'That they are. Split shot.' He put the small tin down on the copper. 'You'll need about three each to make the float stand up.'

During the meal Henry and I talked non-stop about the fishing we would do that afternoon. Henry was always a fast eater, but he must have broken his record that day. I was only halfway through my pudding when he finished, jumped up and went off into the kitchen. Mr Peckover said:

'Hello! He's having a look at his rod.'

I still hadn't finished my pudding when Henry appeared at the door.

'His rod's longer than mine.'

Mr Peckover finished his cup of tea and got up.

'Is it? We'll have a look.'

We filed back into the kitchen and the three of us watched as Mr Peckover held the canes together, and pushed the thick ends into a corner under the sink. We could see that my rod was an inch or two longer than Henry's. Mr Peckover untied my line, took out his penknife and, with a few strokes, cut the end off my cane. He checked the lengths, then tied my line on again.

I decided to compare the length of our lines when nobody was looking, in case Henry's was longer.

We found several jam jars in the pantry, and were already running round

Ken fishing from the stile where he caught 13 gudgeon

to the garden as Mr Peckover cycled off to work. We dug up some worms - the only bait we knew.

As we were setting out Henry said: 'Where can we fish?'

I knew the Long Pond, with all its expert fishermen, was out of the question. We would probably be set upon by a crowd of Lynn boys anyway. But I knew just the place where there were fish, and where there would be nobody about.

'From the stile by Green's shed,' I said.

'Where's that?'

'The Gaywood River. I'll show you.'

We turned left at the Swan Laundry. As we walked along the river I thought of how Mr Peckover had arranged our surprise. He had produced our presents out of his haversack like a conjurer producing a rabbit from a hat. He must have had advice on how to fix on floats and weights because I was sure he didn't know about such things. He must have bought the tackle in Clough's in the High Street. But I couldn't think where he had got the canes. It wasn't until some years later that he told me they came from Humphrey's, a ship's chandler near St Nicholas' Church.

We walked the two hundred yards along My Ditch to where it was fed by water from a dyke at the back of Mill Houses. The stile was only a few feet further on, next to the river. The fence beside it projected several feet out into the water. I showed Henry how to bite the weights on to the gut. With two medium and one large shot the floats stood up perfectly.

We took it in turns to sit at the end of the fence where we could reach over some luxuriant, slow-waving water weeds. We had bites most of the time, from the bank as well as the fence, and we missed a lot more than we caught. The afternoon wore on, and we decided Mrs Peckover would be getting worried. She had no idea where we were. We tied the lines round our canes, and picked up the jam jars as best we could. Every one had fish in it.

It wasn't as late as we thought, and we were home before Mr Peckover.

When he arrived, before he could get off his bike, I leant out of the window.

'I caught thirteen! Henry got one, too!'

Henry, standing just behind me, said: 'You're a show-off.'

He was probably right, but it was so exciting that I might well have said much the same thing if he had caught the thirteen, and I the one.

All the fish were gudgeon. They were beautiful: brown, silver, green and even blue, with dark speckles over body and fins. I soon found out the gudgeon was a member of the carp family, with the Latin name of *gobio gobio*. In one way I was sorry we had caught them, yet it was a wonderful experience to get to know fish, and I felt a great affinity with them. It was all so exciting that I never got round to comparing the lengths of our lines.

Those Foreigners

Although Lynn was a town of over 25,000 people it felt very rural to us Londoners. Just at the back of the Tuesday Market Place was the River Ouse with green fields on the other bank. For me, the country started at the back of Mill Houses with Thurston's field and the dyke. It wasn't very far from our side of Lynn to the Cut Bridge on the opposite side where town once more gave way to countryside. In Lynn itself you could get from very near the centre by way of St James' Park, The Walks and Chase area into open country. From the end of Littleport Street at the Highgate Bridge you could walk through Kettlewell Lane to the Long Pond, and from there all the way to Wootton Road along the river. From there, at the Stone Bridge, you were again very near open country. From the Lily Pond you could cross Peck's Field, go through the allotments and be out on the marshes. Nowhere did we feel far from the country.

Many Lynn people had come from the countryside. Mr Peckover was born in West Winch, then a very small village well outside Lynn. Mrs Peckover was born in the hamlet of Rougham then in Great Massingham, where her father was a gardener. When they first got married they lived in Priory Lane, in the old part of Lynn.

Lynn people spoke in what was for us a country accent. Mr Peckover seldom said 'Yes'. It was always 'Ah'. Many Lynn people who did say 'Yes' pronounced it 'Yis'. The 'I' was pronounced 'Oi', and the 'o', as in 'rose', was pronounced 'rooz'. Lynn people used the word 'that' a lot more than we did because of expressions like 'That oi am' and 'That oi hent'. Pronunciation clearly distinguished Linnets from Londoners.

Another difference was that Lynn people always seemed to know each other or their families. They would often say something like: 'Ah well, she was a Chase before she married. They lived in the grandparents' place in North End. Her brother was a grave-digger and worked at Stanton's.'

One day Mr and Mrs Peckover were talking about a complaint someone had made about meat bought in a shop in town. They knew exactly what the complaint had been, the background of the person who had made it, all her family, and what the shop's reaction had been. Mr Peckover knew even more, and went into a long story of how the man had come to own a butcher's shop, finishing with:

'He ent a proper butcher; just some jumped-up bloke.'

Lynn boys seemed to have a different sense of humour from ours. For example, Tommy Handley's ITMA was not as popular with them as it was with us.

Londoners thought that Lynn people were more boastful. Often, after saying how good he was at something, a Lynn person would add: 'And that's blowing your own trumpet, that is!'

To which the listener often added: 'Well, if you don't blow your own trumpet nobody else will.'

We saw such confidence as dangerous. Boast about something like fighting or running, and you'd be inviting a challenge. It didn't seem to work like that in Lynn, and people would talk about their strong points without fear or embarrassment.

I was later to discover that Lynn people's views of Londoners were surprisingly reciprocal. Of course, Linnets found our accent strange, and wondered why we didn't know each other better. But they also found our sense of humour unsubtle and crude. Even more surprisingly they found Londoners over-confident and boastful. As the war went on I could understand this point of view. After all, the Londoners were the visitors, yet they were very confident and pushy about telling Lynn people how they should go about things in their own town.

Paul Richards, the Lynn historian, says that 'The rough manners and dirty appearance of many London children shocked Lynn's respectable citizens who had known little of the degree of slum life in Britain's large cities.' (*King's Lynn,* Paul Richards, Phillimore 1997) But many Londoners saw things differently. Only a few minutes after arriving we had been shocked by the young boy covered in coal dust, standing on the coal lorry and smoking. There were places in North End that rivalled any slums I knew in East London and, for a long time, I avoided them. I didn't dare enter the Highgate area more than once or twice during the whole war. And the 'Hillen Road Gang' was infamous enough to deter Londoners and Linnets alike from straying on to their territory. Turbus Road was another tough place that many respectable citizens of Lynn knew little about.

Londoners had to beware of situations where they were outnumbered. Not many yards above the Stone Bridge on Wootton Road was a small electricity generating plant where the water was deep, and suitable for swimming and, as I later learnt, for pike. Early in the war half a dozen of us were swimming there when some Lynn boys arrived. They were older than we were, and scowled at us as they got changed. Once in the water they were soon trying to push us under, so we got out, put shoes on, collected our clothes and ran off. They ran after us shouting that they would get us but fortunately we could run faster with shoes on than they could barefoot. We weren't going to get into a fight with boys who outnumbered us and had clumps of dark hair under their armpits!

It is possible that evacuees came from families who were, on average, poorer than the average Lynn family. The seats of London boys' trousers were usually repaired many times before being thrown away or passed on. Repairs were done with circular or oval-shaped pieces of material, so if you saw the 'pair of eyes' on a boy's bottom, you could be pretty sure he was a Londoner.

Especially during the first winter there was another way that Lynn and London boys could be physically distinguished. It was the Balaclava helmets. They were made of leather, with chin straps and ear holes that could be covered over by flaps. That winter practically every Lynn boy wore one, but I never saw any Londoner with one. When you saw a Balaclava, you knew you were looking at a Lynn boy. Perhaps Londoners couldn't afford them. Or perhaps it was because Londoners didn't have their parents on the spot to buy such things for them.

Balaclava helmets were a great advantage to Lynn boys for snowball fights. These took place every other week when we were leaving morning school and they came for the afternoon session. When they were there in the morning they had gone home by the time we arrived but, when we were there in the mornings we waited for their arrival; it was not long, as the school buildings were used as much as possible. We would let the Lynn boys get into their playground at St James' then, armed with two or three snowballs each, we would charge and pen them there. As long as we could contain them we had a ready supply of snow from the grass area in front of the school. But we were always outnumbered. For every snowball we threw, four or five came back, and eventually we would be driven to the other side of the road. There, we had the shelter of trees and shrubs, but very little snow. We were sometimes pinned there for long periods while a constant volley of snowballs came from the hundred or more Lynn boys. If they aimed at the branches above our heads they could send clumps of snow over us. If we peered round a tree trunk we would attract an immediate salvo and, as we dodged back, the Lynn boys cheered and jeered.

It took us a long time to scrape together another two or three snowballs beneath those trees but, when we had got these, we would charge again, occupying the grass for a few minutes before being pushed back again. By the end of each battle, signalled by the school bell, those tree trunks were spattered with blobs of white, most of which were still there the next day.

We were often hit in the face, or had snow down our necks, but the

32

Balaclava helmets were almost complete protection for the Lynn boys. Our strongest weapon was a tough boy named Peter Jackson who seemed impervious to snowballs, and even in the coldest weather never wore more than a shirt and light pullover. He would often charge, all alone, carrying two snowballs, pretending to throw them right and left, putting opponents to flight. Once, without a snowball, head down and whirling a piece of rope in front of him, he rushed all the Lynn boys and put them to flight. It must be admitted he was much bigger than most of them.

I did once manage to penetrate a Balaclava helmet. We had charged, and were pinning the Lynn boys in the playground, occupying the grass and snow area. They were keeping well back and, since we dare not go into the playground, they had time to dodge all our snowballs. I went up to the school wall, well away from the action and, keeping close to the wall and out of sight, went to the corner of the building. I collected a large snowball and lobbed it high over the corner of the building. I peeped round the corner of the building in time to see my snowball land in the face of an unsuspecting Lynn boy just as he was looking slightly upwards. His head disappeared in an explosion of snow, and the last I saw of the poor boy he was bending double, with two or three friends taking off his Balaclava, and removing snow from his face. It was an unlucky blow for him - a lucky one for me.

There was one snowball opponent against whom I never won. He was Jack, a lean, tallish man who had a small poultry farm off Salter's Road, at the back of Raby Avenue. The machine gun post was in one corner of his field. Every time I went there with Mr Peckover that winter, Jack would start a snowball fight. His aim was unerring, and he could reduce a soft snowball to a small, solid, ice-ball in seconds. He always had an ice-ball ready when I needed to bend down to collect snow, and would hit me with it. By the time I had a snowball ready, he had another one himself. I must have hit him only a few times in all the contests we had. What with that, and being butted by the aggressive billy-goat there, those visits were a painful experience.

The snowball fights between Linnets and Londoners were informal, and the result of half-time school. As far as I know there was only ever one organised competition between the two groups, and that was a football match very early on in the war. It was played on Lynn Town's ground at the Walks. I knew none of the Lynn players at the time, but did know something about the London team because they came from my sister's school. There were very few boys to choose from, and only two were interested in football. One was Tommy Miller, known as 'Tufty', who later joined the Loke Road fire-watching group. The other was a boy known as 'Buttons'. He was short, and lightly built, but could dribble, passed well, and had good ball-control. Many of the others didn't normally play, and it was quite a job to fit them up with boots. There was a large crowd - rather more than Lynn Town were getting for matches against visiting forces teams. The vast majority were cheering for the Lynn boys, of course, but they were good-natured and appreciative of any good football. The game was even for a while, and the Lynn team was leading 1-0 at half-time. In the second half Tufty ran almost the length of the pitch, passed to Buttons, who scored. Several other London boys and I were sitting on grass by the touch line and, when the goal was scored, we jumped, rolled over and wrestled in our excitement. Not long before the end, to the delight of the majority of spectators, the Lynn boys scored again, and won 2-1. They ought to have won by a greater margin, having controlled the game, so we were all fairly happy.

A few days later I was in town with Mr Peckover when we met one of his friends. They discussed poultry and rabbits for some time, then the other man noticed me. He looked at Mr Peckover.

'Is this your boy then, Wilf?'

'Well, he's not ours,' said Mr Peckover. 'He's an evacuee.'

'A Londoner!' exclaimed the man. 'They can't play football though, can they?'

As we walked on I told Mr Peckover how the Londoners had had to get a team from 12 to 15 boys. Later on I realised that they had probably never played on grass before. When I had represented my London junior school it had always been on a hard surface. From what I later saw of the Lynn boys I never understood how the Londoners managed to hold them to 2-1.

First Day at the Long Pond

For some weeks after catching those thirteen gudgeon I spent every spare moment along the Gaywood River with my cane, and learnt how to strike properly, how to use a longer piece of line, how to remove a hook and a lot of other things besides. At home I spent all my time looking at fishing tackle catalogues, reading stories written by anglers and looking up the biological background of fish.

Now, what a day this was going to be! Would I catch fish? Would I be noticed? I hoped that nobody would notice me, or that gangs of Lynn boys wouldn't chase me off. I was going to fish in the Long Pond at last. After careful consideration I had decided to start at 'The Boards'. The Boards were at the Loke Road end of the pond in Harecroft Parade, and were put there to prevent the access road crumbling away into the water. They ran for about twenty yards from the end of the pond nearly as far as the first house along. They stood up about three and a half feet out of the water, a foot above the road surface, and were held in place by square-sectioned, horizontal cross-pieces, one just above water level, the other just below ground level. These in turn were held by thick, wooden posts. I had seen boys sitting on the top of the Boards, their feet resting on the horizontal rail, fishing comfortably. Others stood on the bottom rail, just above water level, holding the tops of the boards with one hand, and leaning out over the water with a rod in the other hand.

As far as I was concerned there were several advantages to be had at The Boards. The water was deep, so you could catch fish a very short distance out. It was an easy place to fish from. The place was next to Loke Road, so you could go from there to the pond without having to pass lots of other anglers. If things turned nasty I could make a quick getaway for the same reason. The Boards was a very popular place where you could mingle with all the others, and be inconspicuous. And there seemed to be fish at The Boards all the time.

I left Mill Houses and walked along the Loke, trying to look both nonchalant and professional - a seasoned Long Ponder. When I reached the pond I nearly lost my nerve and turned back. Boys were fishing elbow to elbow, lines were being thrown out and pulled in, and there was a buzz of conversation. Realising just in time that these were the conditions I really wanted, I walked past the railings amongst the anglers, looking for a place. A space opened up, I stepped into it, put my toes against the boards, and tossed my line out. Almost immediately the float bobbed, and moved sideways. I struck, and caught a gudgeon! I removed the hook, put the fish gently back into the water and, aware that boys on both sides were watching me, cast out again. I soon had another bite, struck, but missed. Then I had a different sort of bite, and caught a small roach, about the same size as the gudgeon. I had bites, and caught a fish every few minutes for some time. Then a boy on my right looked at me and said:

'Coo! You're catching a lot!' I had been spoken to! In a friendly way! At the Long Pond!

I said: 'There must be lots of fish here. How many have you caught?'

The boy, younger than I had first thought, said: 'Three. But my bait's too soft. It keeps coming off.'

'What is it?' I asked. He showed me. It was flour mixed with water. It must have been coming off as it went down through the water. I said:

'I'm fishing with dead worm. Do you want a piece of it?'

'Don't you catch eels with that?' I didn't tell him I'd never caught an eel.

'Well, I'm catching gudgeon, roach and dace. At least a bit of worm stays on.'

'Can you put it on for me?'

I did, and he began fishing again, catching more than he had been before.

For some time I had been aware of a voice from behind. It couldn't be anything to do with me, so I took no notice. But the voice persisted:

'Hey! Look over here!'

Eventually I glanced behind.

'Here! Come over here!' I saw a garden fence with a bit of trellis and, in one of the trellis gaps was a small face.

'Yes! You! Come over here!'

It was a young boy shouting at me! I propped my rod on the Boards and went over. A stick, held by a boy of about four years, was poked through the trellis.

'Will you put a point on my stick, please?'I took out my penknife and began cutting at one end. I thought I'd better do the job properly, and finished with a very sharp point. The boy was dancing about in his excitement, pulled the stick back, and pushed another one through.

'Can you do my brother's stick, please?'

There was now an even smaller boy, only about two years old, standing there. As I hacked away at his stick he looked on, wide-eyed, following every movement of the penknife. When I had made another good point I handed it to him. The two boys ran off, up the garden, whooping and brandishing their pointed sticks. I went back to my rod and carried on fishing. Then another boy, about five or six, came up to me holding a short cane.

Ken with a young angler at the Long Pond

'Can you put my bait on for me?' He handed me his hook. It was a bent pin, but bent once, in the middle, at about 120°. It wasn't hook-shaped at all. He was about as likely to catch a fish with that as with a straight pin. I asked:

'Have you ever caught a fish with this hook?'

'Not yet,' he said.

Using the top of the Boards I pushed the pin's point a lot nearer the head, making it more like a hook. Then I took a piece of the boy's bait, worked it a bit, then squeezed it on to the point.

'Are you coming this afternoon?'

'Yes,' replied the boy.

'If you bring your hook along I'll bend it into a proper hook shape with some pliers.' The boy looked puzzled. 'Some pliers,' I said.

The boy obviously didn't understand so, using Mr Peckover's expression, and his way of talking, I said: 'A pair o' nippers.'

He understood! My first serious attempt at the Norfolk language had been successful! In the same vein I asked:

'Would you loik a fish with moi rard?'

His face lit up, and he took my cane. After less than half a minute he began getting a bite, but struck a bit too early. He had four or five more bites then, still too early I thought, struck and caught a roach. He shouted at the top of his voice telling everyone around that he had caught a fish. I unhooked it for him, and it was only after I assured him that he'd catch more fish that he reluctantly agreed to put the fish back. Soon after that, boys began drifting away, so I stuck the hook into the bottom of the cane, wound the line tight round the top, and went homewards along the Loke. What a success! I had fished at the Long Pond. I had *caught* fish at the Long Pond. Most important of all, I was accepted at the Long Pond, even if only by very young anglers so far.

Over a hurried meal I told my hosts about the fish I had caught, and what a wonderful place the Long Pond was. Mr Peckover looked doubtful when I asked him about the pliers, and wanted to know why I needed them. When I explained, he went out to the shed and came back with an old pair I had never seen before.

'Don't you go a-losin' on 'em.'

When I got back to the pond there weren't any anglers about, but I decided to play safe and take the same place as in the morning. The fish were biting just as well, and the Boards began to fill up. It wasn't long before the boy came up with his half-bent pin. It wasn't easy but, by using the pliers and a kerb behind us, I did manage to give the pin a reasonable hook shape. I put a piece of dead worm on it and the boy began fishing beside me. He got a bite immediately, and caught several fish that afternoon. He was delighted enough to agree to put the fish back each time.

Before long I heard the voice coming from behind again, so put my rod down and went to the fence. The elder boy thrust another stick towards me, asking for a point. When that was done, the smaller one pushed another stick out, and I put a point on that, too. I asked them what their names were. The elder was David, and the younger was Robert. They went running off, as before, waving their pointed sticks. I didn't think to ask them what had happened to the sticks they had in the morning.

A boy of about my own age asked me why I was using worm.

'Bread's a lot better.'

When I asked him how bread bait was made, he gave a very clear description. You break a slice of bread into crumbs, put them in a piece of rag, twist the sides of the rag until the crumbs are trapped tightly, dip this into water and squeeze again.

His bread was firm, and stayed on the hook very well. He insisted on giving me a piece of his bait, so I used it, and began catching fish even more quickly than with the piece of worm.

Fishing side by side we couldn't avoid having our floats only inches apart at times. When you hauled out, you might not be able to put it back in the same place because another float would be there. During the afternoon I was surprised to see my float suddenly dive out of sight. I struck, but it hadn't been a bite. Another young angler's line had caught around mine and, when he struck, he had pulled my float downwards. The boy immediately shouted:

'Firsty cut!'

I had heard that several times before, and now learnt that it meant the other boy had the right to do a cut first if we couldn't undo the tangle. In fact, tangles were usually sorted out amicably, as was that one, and it was to be a year or more before I saw a line cut.

More frequent was the shout: 'Garim!'

This simply meant 'got him!', but it was rather more frequent, at times, than the rate at which fish were being caught, because boys tended to shout it before they had pulled the fish out, or even before they had hooked it. Some of them said it as they struck!

That afternoon two other people spoke to me. One was a man, who asked: 'Are they biting?'

The other was a boy, who asked: 'Caught any?'

As I went back along the Loke later that afternoon, proudly carrying my cane, I thought of all the wonderful things that had happened that day. What an eventful morning and afternoon! What a marvellous place the Long Pond was!

During the following weeks, spending every available minute at the Long Pond, I got to know more kinds of fish, more anglers and more neighbours.

I caught gudgeon, roach, dace, silver bream, bleak and carp. And I discovered there were monster carp and pike there. Occasionally one of these would jump, making a splash as loud as a brick landing in the water from a great height.

David and Robert Rose, from the garden by the Boards, lived in the corner house, 'Kano', with their mother and grandmother. Their father had been called up and was abroad. Their home was really off Tennyson Avenue, but they were living with the grandmother for the duration of the war. It was a typical family of the time.

There was another younger boy who lived by the pond. He was Neville, and lived at No. 1, right at the far end of Harecroft Parade. What a wonderful place to live! On one side was the railway, with its wild embankment. Right in front, only a few feet away, was the Long Pond. If I had lived there I would have fished from an upstairs window. Had I then known all the advantages of living in that house I would have been even more envious.

I had also got to know a lot of dogs. Young anglers brought them along, and they were as friendly as the anglers themselves. They wagged their tails when you stroked them or offered them bread bait, and even when you just spoke to them.

Being at the Long Pond was different. It wasn't like the rest of the world. And here, everyone was a Linnet. All the talk was about fish and fishing, and it was done in a Norfolk accent. Long Pond life was separate from the rest of life. Here were the 'different' Lynn boys. They also loved fish and fishing. I now understood those 'foreigners'.

Henry Goes

Firewood was needed much of the year at 23 Mill Houses for the open fire, and all year round for Mrs Peckover's weekly copper wash, so chopping wood went on regularly. Unchopped wood was stacked round the inside walls of the bike shed, and chopped wood was taken upstairs and put with the coal. Both Henry and I loved chopping so when, one day, Mrs Peckover asked us to do some, we rushed downstairs to get on with it. We moved the bikes out first, because it was much more satisfying to chop on the loose-brick floor than on the garden path. Henry had reached the axe first, so he started chopping while I stacked. This went on for a long time and I eventually decided it was my turn.

'Come on! You've had a good innings!'

'Hang on! I'll just finish these bits!' He finished those bits, and started some more. I began counting to myself.

'That's ten more! My turn now!'

'It wasn't ten!'

'Yes it was! And now that's ten more!'

'Course it's not!'

'Look! She won't want much more than this,' I complained. 'There's nearly enough to fill up the coal hole!' I began counting out loud. 'Forty! Forty-one! Forty-two!' Then: 'Fifty more!'

Henry stood up, kicked a piece of wood at my shins, and rushed at me, the axe upraised. I didn't think for a moment he would dare hit me with an axe, but wasn't going to take any chances. I managed to grab his arm, twist it, and wrestled him to the ground. Henry began punching and kicking but, seeing the axe was lying in a corner, I gave him a push. He fell against the stacked wood and I rushed out of the shed slamming the door behind me. I sprinted along the garden path, vaulted the gate and was running past Ted Mindham's back door when the axe hit Ted's gate with a loud clonk! A piece of wood flew upwards. I shouted: 'Ha! Ha! Missed!' and ran off round the corner of the house block. Henry didn't give chase, and I went off for an hour or two.

When I got back, Mr Peckover was home from work and knew all about the incident. Mrs Peckover had seen it from the back window, and they had already decided Henry had to go. I told them what I am sure was the truth:

that he wouldn't have hit me with the axe and, when he threw it, he aimed to miss. It was the sort of thing we did. But they had made up their minds.

Henry had gone within a couple of days to a childless couple in Austin Street. The husband was an ex-boxer, but a very gentle man who liked children. He and his wife took Henry about a lot, and tried to get him to settle with them. But he didn't stay long, and was one of the many evacuees who, having once changed billet, soon returned to London.

A week or two later I was getting some weights out of a tin and came across a blue and white float. Henry had left his fishing tackle behind, so I now had two floats! Mr Peckover had put Henry's cane in the garden so, one day when nobody was about, I went down to look for it. I found it leaning against the greenhouse and did casting and striking movements with it. It didn't feel like a proper rod, so I put it back.

About that time my sister's hosts decided they wouldn't have an evacuee any more. When Mr and Mrs Peckover heard this they offered to take her. She was four years older than I was, and was leaving school at the end of the following term, so it wasn't for long. But it meant less comfortable sleeping arrangements for me: the chaise-longue with a chair at the end. One evening Mrs Peckover put one of Joan's vests on the door of the open fire to warm it up. Somehow the vest got shut inside the oven and there was a strong smell of burning. Mrs Peckover rushed to rescue the garment, but it was burnt to a cinder. I assumed it was a disaster, but our hosts were helpless with laughter. We were soon laughing with them.

Ken, his sister
Joan, and
Gyp and pup

Don't Want to Go Home

Although my hosts' movements were mainly for purposes like work, shopping, visiting friends or viewing poultry and rabbits, they did sometimes cycle or walk for pleasure. Often, on a Sunday, they walked along the Gaywood River, always surprised at the number and size of the roach there. But I don't think they had ever been over the marshes, and they hardly ever went past the Long Pond.

One day, when I was extolling those two places, and telling Mr and Mrs Peckover what they were missing, Mr Peckover looked up and asked:

'Don't you want to go home, then?'

I did long to go home, and hoped the war would be very short. Every time I thought of home I got a pang in the pit of my stomach. But at the same time I did know there were some marvellous places here, in Lynn. The question had come as a surprise, and I didn't like to say I wanted to leave. So I simply answered:

'No.'

After that, whenever we were with other people, Mr Peckover would tell them: 'He don't want to go home.' Then, looking at me: 'Do you, Ken?'

For a long time I said I didn't want to go home, but felt more and more uneasy, even guilty, about it. One day my answer came out as: 'Well, not really.' This gradually changed to: 'Well, in many ways, no', or: 'Well, in some ways I don't.'

Eventually I was qualifying even more: 'Well, it's hard to say. There isn't a Long Pond, or Gaywood River, or proper marshes in London.' This was my stock answer for a long time, and often caused some amusement. But I still felt uneasy about it.

One day I was with Mr and Mrs Peckover in town when we met a family they knew well. At one point in the conversation Mr Peckover said: 'He don't want to go home, do you, Ken?'

This time I replied: 'Well, I'd be silly not to want to go home, wouldn't I?'

I regretted saying it immediately. There was a short silence, then other things were talked about. Mr Peckover never asked me that question again.

Where is My Ditch ?

Coming out of St James' school one week when we were on the afternoon session I went home through The Walks and Tennyson Avenue. Approaching the Swan Laundry Bridge by the river bank on the other side of My Ditch, bending low to keep out of sight of fish, I crept towards Salter's Road.

41

A recent photo of the much narrower Gaywood River from the Swan Laundry Bridge. The black bullock stands on the line of 'My Ditch' now filled in.

Although looking out for fish, I was aware of something different about the other side. No sedges or reeds were blowing about in the wind. I ran over the bridge, and down the other side. The sedges and reeds were indeed gone! So was My Ditch! It had been filled in with soil and stones! I ran to the far end. All two hundred yards of ditch had suffered the same fate. Not an inch had been spared. I rushed off to tell Mr and Mrs Peckover.

'Who did it?' I shouted. 'I knew all those creatures! Thousands of them! People who do that ought to be buried alive themselves!'

My hosts thought the only people who could give permission to fill in a ditch would be 'The Corporation'. Mr Peckover said he was sure there must be a good reason for any infilling, but I argued that there should be laws against burying alive things like sticklebacks, leeches, frogs and, for that matter, insects and plants.

Over the following weeks I tried to find anyone who could tell me why such a thing had been done. I spoke to anglers, teachers, neighbours, friends and parents of friends. Nobody had an explanation. Nobody had noticed, and nobody was concerned.

There had always been a narrow, cockleshell footpath between the Gaywood River and My Ditch. It was now suddenly wider, and one or two cars began using it to get to some sheds further along. That was my first experience of 'development'.

Not long ago I found out someone else had noticed, and had been concerned about the destruction of My Ditch. That was well over half a century later.

Changing Schools

One morning I paused at the gate of St James' school building. Why was I still here, at Rochelle Street? Changing schools should be easy. So I walked fifty yards further on, and turned into the London Secondary School.

Inside the playground I was surrounded by some big boys in long trousers who asked me if I was a new boy. I told them I was. When a bell sounded they all began lining up in classes, and a teacher came out. I kept out of sight of the teacher and, when he went inside, I followed. The teacher was at the bottom of some stairs, and saw me come in. When he asked me what I was doing there I gave him what must have been an incomprehensible summary of my reasons. He took me up two flights of stairs, and off to the right into a room marked 'Headmaster'. I told the headmaster my story, and how old I was, and he seemed to understand. He knew my name because my sister had left the school not long before. But he was non-committal, and the other teacher later accompanied me back to the junior school. The junior school headmistress was furious, and kept me in her office for much of the morning telling me how wicked I was. When I went back to join my class they were having a lesson with Mr Taylor. As I sat down at the back, he shouted:

'Well, Regelous, are you in this school or not?'

I said I didn't know.

The next day the headmistress, Miss Isles, began a series of visits to 23, Mill Houses, trying to convince Mrs Peckover that I should remain at the school. There was no need to go on to the other school because her junior school was going to 'become a secondary school'. They were just about to start French and algebra. Mrs Peckover always took the line that any decision about which school I went to should be my mother's. There was one French lesson, but it was part of an English lesson and didn't last long. We didn't do any algebra at all.

Worms

Near where we lived in London was an old church in rambling grounds and surrounded by a high wall. That was the only place around where I sometimes saw earthworm casts and, occasionally, a worm itself. My grandfather, who lived in a small two-up and two-down, had a small back yard partly cultivated, and I sometimes asked him if he ever found worms there. He always said:

'You see one or two.'

I often scratched around there, never seeing one worm, let alone two.

In Lynn there were worms everywhere. You could see casts all over the garden and allotment, even on the ash paths. They were in all the front and back gardens of Mill Houses, and in the spaces between blocks. They were often stranded on pavements, in roads and puddles, and I rescued them, putting them back into soil. You had only to pull up a clod of grass at the Long Pond to find one. At the Saunders, by the sluice gate, was a brick flotsam bin where council men put what they collected from the nearby flotsam trap. Here were thousands and thousands of red worms which lots of anglers used for bait. Worms often fell, wriggling, into the pond, and we would try to rescue them. I even found drowned worms in the old copper; goodness knows how they got in there!

Worms were the only bait I knew of until I started to fish at the Long Pond, and it wasn't long before I had taken over a patch of garden about twelve feet by six as a wormery. It was beside a shed, and didn't get too dry, but I nevertheless watered it regularly and dug in old vegetables or manure. After I stopped using live worms I found that dead ones from puddles or the copper were almost as good.

I was fishing in the Long Pond one day when a Lynn boy I knew came along with his sister who, in the course of conversation, asked me what I was using for bait. I told her it was a piece of boiled potato. She screwed up her face.

'That's what *people* eat! You should be fishing with worms.'

I said that people and animals often eat the same thing. The girl ignored this.

'Worms are better, and anyway people don't eat them.'

'Yes, they do,' I argued. 'Some people in South America eat worms *and* maggots. I don't use them now because it's cruel.'

I thought she was going to point out that hooking fish was cruel as well, but she snapped:

'*You* don't eat worms, I bet!'

She said it so confidently that I couldn't resist saying I had eaten one or two worms in the past.

'All right,' said the girl, 'I'll get a worm. Eat it and prove it!'

'I don't eat *raw* worms,' I argued. 'Do you eat raw potatoes?'

She didn't answer this question. 'What do you do then, fry them?'

Not knowing much about cooking I agreed they were fried.

'So if I get a worm, you'd fry it and eat it?'

I agreed, feeling fairly safe she wasn't going to produce a frying pan and fire there and then.

'And isn't frying worms cruel?'

'Of course it is,' I said, 'that's why I've stopped eating them.'

I thought that a brilliant answer, and for a moment the girl looked puzzled. 'So you'd put them in your mouth, you mean, but not eat them?'

For some reason I said 'Yes', whereupon the girl rushed up the bank followed by her brother, and they both began pulling out clods of grass.

They rejected the first few worms on the grounds that they were too small, and finally chose one that, whilst nowhere near a night gobbler*, was about three inches long. The girl offered it to me.

'There's one. Put that in your mouth then!'

Making sure they could see it wasn't a trick, I put the worm straight in, and shut my mouth over it. I still remember the distinctive taste of that worm as it wriggled about. The boy and his sister looked horrified and moved back up the bank. I left the worm in for some seconds then took it out, put it back with the clods of grass and covered it over.

I did my worm-in-the-mouth act twice more, once in front of a delighted and appreciative audience of young anglers at the Saunders, and once in St James' Park for a couple of girls. Then someone told me worms had lots of parasites crawling all over them. I lost my nerve, and never repeated the performance.

The Lynn boy who had been with his sister did sometimes fish at the Long Pond himself, and he was there a week or two later with his cane. When I asked him what he'd caught he made a face.

'Nothin', but I'm not really interested in fishin'. It's borin'.'

I'd never heard that from an angler before.

'But you never know when you're going to get a bite. And when you do, you don't know what it is. There could be big 'uns round your bait this very minute.'

He pulled out his line. 'See! My bait's gone. I bet it fell off.'

He felt in a pocket and I thought he was going to bring out some bait. But instead he took out a reel.

'I've had this weeks and can't be bothered to put it on.'

It was made of black bakelite, about two inches across with two small handles. No ratchet, but just the sort of thing I had been looking for.

'D'you want to sell it then?'

He looked willing. 'What would you give me for it?'

I didn't know what to guess at. All the money I owned at that moment was threepence, which I had with me.

'I'll give you threepence.'

He handed the reel over and I paid quickly in case he changed his mind. I rushed home and fixed it on to my cane with rubber washers from pop bottles. I already had a top ring and three rod rings of the snake variety. Mr Peckover tied these on with snobbing twine by his 'knotless' method, and gave me twenty yards of the same twine which filled up the reel.

What a difference that reel would make! I could now get out into the middle and fish for 'big 'uns'. Almost as good was putting the hook through the lowest rod ring, holding the cane by the middle and walking around showing it off.

I thought it was a bargain; but perhaps my friend meant it as a reward for my worm trick.

* A very large earth worm

The Flea that Gave Itself Up

Some years before the war, when I got home one afternoon, my mother asked me not to go near the sewing machine. It was enough to make anyone curious, and I soon spotted a furry ball crouching under the treadle. We had a kitten! It was very timid, and it was some time before we could pick it up, but I did eventually manage to pick it up and stroke its white neck. It was then I saw a small, dark object, that moved rapidly down into the fur, out of sight. The kitten had fleas. One day, alone indoors, I managed to pick out a score or more fleas, and put them on the table with a plate over them. I rushed out, found my mother, and told her what I had done. When we went back, only a few minutes later, all the fleas had disappeared. Eventually, with hard work and liberal applications of Keating's powder, we got rid of the fleas.

The nearest cat to 23 Mill Houses belonged to Mr Bailey, a widower who lived in number 21, below us on the other side. It didn't seem to have a name, and we always called it 'Old Bailey's cat'. I used to sit at the bottom of the stairs for hours with Old Bailey's cat on my lap, stroking it. I often looked for fleas, but never found any. I made friends with lots of other Lynn cats, and looked for fleas, but they all seemed flea-free.

Mr Peckover came up from the garden one evening, and removed his shirt and vest. He had never done that before. Mrs Peckover began picking at his back and chest. When I asked what was happening she explained:

'He's been plucking a couple of chickens and I'm just taking some fleas off him.'

She laughed as I quickly went to the other side of the room.

'It's all right! They're not human fleas. I get them off because they're itchy.'

I supposed they must be like cat fleas, and not at home on humans.

I was still at the junior school when Mrs Peckover noticed the headlice. They were glinting in the sunlight on my hair. As soon as she said the word 'lice' I realised I had been feeling itchy for some time. There followed a period of weeks when Mrs Peckover spent hours every evening combing them out. One day, in the classroom, I felt one going down the back of my neck, managed to get it between finger and thumb, and put it into an inkwell. Being in that school, and having lice, was probably the lowest point of my evacuation. Eventually, as a result of Mrs Peckover's regular combings, I was rid of them, and never had any again. There was a plague of them at the time, something I had never known in London. Most of the Londoners didn't know the word 'lice'. They talked about 'lights', and went around asking people if they had 'lights' in their hair, then roaring with laughter.

Mr Peckover had a favourite dish that I had never seen before. He would cut off a piece of cheese, break it into small pieces on his plate, pour on vinegar, and mash it up with a fork. On top of that went a sprinkling of salt.

He often had this to finish off his tea or supper, and it wasn't long before I copied him.

One afternoon I decided to finish up with this luxury and, in the process of putting on the vinegar, must have left a spot high up on the side of the plate. I had almost finished eating when something landed on the spot of vinegar. I thought it was some kind of fly. One side seemed to be stuck to the vinegar, and it began pushing itself rapidly round with its free leg, the drop of vinegar as centre of a circle.

As I stared, Mr Peckover exclaimed. He had seen it happen too, although further along the table. Even more surprising was that Mrs Peckover, right at the end of the table, had also seen it.

'That's a flea!' she said.

She jumped up, took the plate, and crushed the creature with her thumbnail.

We always referred to it as the flea that gave itself up.

The First One-day Wonder

The faces we saw at the Long Pond, whether of anglers or passers-by, were usually familiar ones. Occasionally somebody new appeared, and caused a stir, but most of these went off never to be seen again.

The first one-day wonder was, to us, elderly, although he may well have been under fifty. I was fishing at the concrete end, and saw him arrive through the kissing-gates, pushing his bike. He didn't look around to choose where to fish, but stopped at the first empty space, not far from directly opposite the Tunmores' house. He put his bike against the railings, climbed over, and began untying his rod from the crossbar. He looked very confident as he looked around at the young anglers. We didn't have many adults fishing at the pond, and several pairs of young eyes were on him as he flourished his 3-joint rod, and put on a large reel. We could see by his heavy line that he wasn't interested in little 'uns. He threaded his line through the rod rings and then, instead of putting on a float, took out an artificial worm about a foot long. Made of red, rubber piping, with two large trebles, it was bigger than the biggest fish most of us had caught. We were going to see something special today!

He was a very thin man, not very tall and with a permanent smile. As he tackled up he chatted non-stop to the growing number of anglers around him. He tied on his huge, artificial bait, and prepared to cast out. He pulled his line off the reel, and let it lie on the grassy bank in front of him. There was enough line to go most of the way across the pond. Perhaps he was going to cast at an angle, up towards the Point. Then he swung the rod round, just missing the hedge behind. There was a loud swish and to our disappointment the heavy artificial bait came down with a splash only a few yards out, and there was a massive tangle at his bottom ring, as well as line still in the long grass at his feet.

Undaunted and still smiling, he put his rod against the railings and began undoing his tangle, chatting to the young anglers around him. By the time he had undone all his knots, and wound in the line, several pedestrians had stopped to watch. I moved a bit nearer to hear more easily what he was saying.

'Ah well, that's sorted out. Not seen gear like this before, have you? Did my worm frighten you? I don't go after tiddlers. We'll soon find out what there is in here.'

As he wound in, his line tightened. He pulled, but it wouldn't come out. A dozen young voices shouted:

'You're hooked in the wood, mister!'

We all knew there was some submerged boarding about eight feet out. The other side of this the depth suddenly increased, and it was there that several young anglers had been fishing when the newcomer came along.

He pulled this way and that, climbed back over the rails and walked several yards towards the Loke, pulling hard.

'Won't come out that way! Let's try from over there!'

He went towards the kissing-gates, still tugging. Some of the young anglers suggested he should walk round the pond and pull from the other side but, instead, he climbed back over the railings. A lot more passers-by, several on bikes, had stopped to watch, and there were now as many passers-by as anglers.

Then the man sat down and began removing socks and shoes. Young anglers began shouting.

'It's too deep mister! You sink in the mud! There's a sudden drop there, mister, Your worm's four feet down!'

The man kept smiling. 'That don't matter.'

He removed his pullover, and kept on talking as he took off his shirt. Then he began removing his trousers.

There was a stampede of young anglers as they abandoned fishing and gathered round. More adults were now watching, and there were no more passers-by - they were all stopping.

The man stood up in his long johns. Then he removed his teeth and, still smiling, put them in a trouser pocket. His face looked even thinner than before.

'We'll soon get it back!'

Using feet, hands and bottom he slithered down the bank. Standing in two feet of water he got hold of his line and went slowly out. When he got to the submerged boards he was standing nearly up to his bottom. He put a foot carefully forward.

'Here's your woodwork!' He bent at the knees, feeling downwards along the line until he was crouching so low that the water was up to his chin.

Several young anglers' voices rang out: 'It's too low down, mister!'

He stood up, held his nose, and jumped outwards, disappearing with a splash, amidst exclamations and a few cheers from the now large crowd on both banks. Then a head reappeared, and he stood, water up to his armpits. He was still smiling.

'We'll get it this time.'

He took a deep breath, and disappeared again. Bubbles rose to the surface through what had become almost black water. There were now windows opening in houses on both sides of the pond.

He was under for some time, then his head came up slowly and a jet of water spurted from his mouth. He held up his huge, artificial worm.

'Here we are!'

There were more cheers and claps from the crowd. Everyone was smiling. Holding the line, the man swung the bait towards the bank.

'Look after it, will you?'

A young angler grabbed the rod, and began reeling in. Another got hold of the line. He waited for the man to climb out but, instead, he began doing a backstroke. Out in the middle he turned and made for the far end of the pond.

'Got cups for this! Keep it up all day!'

Young anglers, of whom I was one, ran along, keeping up with him. Reaching the shallow water by the Loke, he sat for a moment, hair and shoulders covered in froth and slimy, green weed that always collected there. He looked down at his arms.

'Have to clean that off!'

Turning himself round he went into a breast stroke, then changed to a rapid crawl, and was soon past the Point and back, opposite his rod. I had never seen crowds like it at the Long Pond before. Our visitor clambered up the bank, grabbed his shirt, and stood there, wiping himself.

'Warmer in than out!'

His long johns were hanging down, a large gap down the front. There were one or two shrieks. The man took no notice, and looked around.

'Never swam in warmer water! Downright hot! Always feel better for a swim!'

With his long johns still streaming with water, and the gap still down the front, he retrieved his teeth, put on shirt, trousers, pullover, socks and shoes, and began dismantling his rod, still muttering cheerfully. He didn't bother to tie the rod back on his crossbar, but held it as he pushed his bike towards the kissing gates. Several youngsters followed him along, and the last we heard was:

'Better get dried off! Couldn't leave it there, could I?'

The only time we hadn't heard him talking was when he was under water.

The man was only halfway across the lines when Les Marriot, an evacuee billeted in Loke Road, shouted across the pond:

'Did you see it?'

That man was the only person we ever saw swim in the Long Pond, and he never came back.

The Pike

One summer's afternoon four Lynn boys and I decided to fish for sticklebacks. One of the best places was in a field the other side of the stile where Henry and I had first gone fishing with canes. Fortunately it was the near side of the next stile. On the other side was a field thick with four- to five-feet-high grasses and, among them, 'courting couples'; we didn't like to venture there, and kept to the footpath.

Our destination was a small pool only about twenty-five feet long, and little more than ten feet wide. It stretched from near the stile to the Rope Walk fence. In wet weather it went past the stile and joined the river itself. Even in summer it had over a foot of depth, was clean and clear, with clumps of healthy-looking water weeds. It was another beautiful place.

We arrived, armed with nets and jars, took off our shoes and socks, and rolled up our short trousers. We stayed there all the afternoon, and must have trodden three-quarters of the bottom. When we came out, the water was dark brown. We ran around for a while, drying off, dressed and returned the sticklebacks. As we were walking away I happened to glance back. There, in the water we had been paddling in all afternoon, a huge green shape broke the surface, moved to the side, and lay still in the shallow water.

I shouted, and rushed back, picking up a stout branch that happened to be lying on the grass. Then I did an awful thing. I hit the green object hard. I had no idea what it was. It shot forward in the water, and turned over. Then we saw that it was a pike. We took it in turns to try to revive it, but it was dead. We were all excited, and I managed to carry it home, followed by the others. Mr Peckover had never seen such a large fish; he weighed it with his spring balance, and it was just over eleven pounds.

That evening, when Mr Peckover put some string through the fish's gills, I took it along Loke Road to the Long Pond, showing it to passers-by and anglers. Mrs Peckover soaked it in vinegar, cooked it, and we ate it between us.

Even as I had hit the poor fish I had pangs of conscience, and these had grown as I had carried it home, and shown it off at the pond. But it was after we had eaten it that I was stricken with horror. How could I have carried out

50

such a cruel and unfeeling act? Why had I done it? The fish must have been frightened for hours while we were there, trampling that small stretch of water. If only I hadn't glanced behind when we were leaving. If only that branch hadn't been there. If only I had looked before hitting it. If only I could have turned the clock back!

We never found out how the pike had got there. It might have been caught by an angler, and put in there. It could have got in from the Gaywood River when the water was high.

That pool lasted for a few years more, getting gradually smaller. Then it disappeared. The reason was almost certainly the ever-declining level of the Gaywood River.

As far as the 11-pound pike is concerned, it is a story I would like to forget. But I know I never shall.

Relative Affluence

Mr and Mrs Peckover often talked about people who were making fortunes because of war. Shopkeepers, farmers, dockers, manufacturers, fishermen and many others had doubled, trebled or quadrupled their incomes.

I reckoned I had done better than all of these.

Mother with Gyp and pup

Before the war my sister and I each had one penny a week for pocket-money: the Saturday penny. I often intended to spend it on an Oxo cube or, even better, a pennyworth of mustard pickles at the grocer's shop on the corner, but I never did because that would have meant using the whole penny in one go, whereas it could be made to last several days. Even a farthing would buy a couple of liquorice sticks. We did get other money at Christmas and birthdays, and always managed to save for our annual two-week holiday at the seaside.

But I felt much better off in Lynn. For one thing, my mother sent a weekly parcel of chocolates and sweets, all costing much more than a penny. With it was a copy of *Adventure*, a boys' weekly magazine.

51

This had stories about Colwyn Dane, the detective; Rockfist Rogan, the RAF boxer; Wild Young Dirky, a Scottish boy who lived in the Highlands, never went to school, and threw knives unerringly enough to gain his livelihood and Red Fury, an American Indian whose ambition was to become heavyweight boxing champion of the world, and who had an Irish trainer whose vocabulary was limited to 'Begorrah'. All this must have increased my income tenfold.

For another thing I still received some pocket-money, and even this was supplemented by the money I got for the children's cinema on Saturday mornings. There was the choice of the Majestic or the Pilot. They were both excellent value, and included a film, a cartoon and a serial, each instalment leaving the heroes in an impossible situation.

These shows were patronised almost entirely by boys. A younger sister might occasionally be brought along, but not often. The films were mainly about cowboys and Indians, detectives or space travellers, with fighting, shooting and chasing which we watched with bated breath. But as soon as the excitement slackened we began talking, then shouting, then whistling. Should a male character look at, or speak to, a female with the slightest tenderness the shouting and whistling became deafening, and foot-stamping shook the building. If ever there was a kiss, the pandemonium would be such that the film would usually be stopped. This only resulted in even louder shouting that we wanted our money back. Sometimes, when a film was stopped, one of the cinema staff would come on to the stage to reason with the audience. They were usually shouted down. Once, at the Pilot, Mr Culey had a film stopped, and came on to the stage, but couldn't make himself heard. One boy roared out:

'Heil Hitler!'

Mr Culey was so incensed that he managed to make himself heard.

'I'll give you bloody heil Hitler!'

Shouts, jeers and loud laughter continued for so long that the man had eventually to leave the stage, unheard except for those six words.

Early on in the war I even managed to afford some stink bombs; the first time ever. That morning, some friends and I were looking for somewhere to throw them. For good effect they needed to be let off in a confined space and, as we went along the High Street we thought Boots shop would be a good target. We went to the entrance, opened the door, hurled stink bomb after stink bomb anywhere inside, and ran off. A few minutes later we met a friend in Norfolk Street and told him what we'd done, and waited while he went off to see what the shop was like. He came back with a vivid description of how the whole place stank, and we decided to go back and see for ourselves. Pretending we were innocent passers-by we took it in turns to peep through the door and, when it was my turn, I saw people with brushes and buckets, and a group of young, female staff were standing in a circle looking at where one stink bomb had hit the side of a counter and dribbled its contents on to the floor. I couldn't resist pushing open the door and throwing several more bombs inside. As I turned to run I was grabbed by an errand boy some four or five years older than I. As we grappled on the pavement I could see this boy's face screwed up in hatred. He gasped:

'Bloody Londoners!'

I thought I was just about getting out of his grip when I was grabbed by a man. The two of them dragged me inside the shop door, then the man, holding me firmly by the arm, said:

'Go and fetch a policeman.' The errand boy rushed off.

I was sure I'd be taken off to the police station and recognised because I had already been in trouble with the police in London. My friend, Don Nicholson, and I had bought some table tennis balls at our nearest Woolworths but when we tried to use them we found over half of them were cracked. We returned to the Woolworths and asked for our money back but, although we saw the same young lady who had served us, and a man who seemed to be in charge of that section, they refused to return our money or change the balls. We were so indignant that we went around taking things from counters and putting them into our pockets. Two men grabbed us and took us to an office at the back, and looked at what we had stolen. It must have been an Easter time because we both had several soft, yellow chicks. There had been a court case about it.

All this went through my mind as I stood there, held by the man. He was dressed in a smart suit, so I imagined he was the manager. People were walking past on the pavement just outside, and I wished I was there with them. A man was standing just outside the door looking in my direction. He was quite short, but stocky, and dressed in ragged clothes rather like a tramp. He was mouthing something at me, then went through a series of movements, sticking out a leg, jerking it back and pushing out with his hands. Then he jerked a thumb off to his left. He walked off a few yards, came back, and did the same things again.

He was encouraging me to trip up the man holding me, and make a run for it! Had he seen which way the errand boy had run off to find a policeman? I looked at the man holding me. He wasn't very tall, and quite slim, but could I possibly get away from him? The man outside was again thumbing off to his left, but more frantically. Was it already too late?

I nodded at the man outside, put my right foot quickly behind the man holding me and shoved as hard as I could. He went backwards and I lunged to the door, opened it, and was outside. The other man was just in front of me, brushing me aside. As I rushed away he did a sort of stagger into the doorway.

'Hey! What's the big hurry?'

I heard the manager trying to get past the man, put my head down, and ran. Within seconds I had passed the end of Norfolk Street and was in the

Tuesday Market Place. I was wearing plimsolls and could run at my maximum speed. I sprinted past the Duke's Head Hotel wondering what I would do if confronted by a policeman. I passed St Nicholas' Church, went down North Street, past the Pilot cinema, over the railway lines and didn't stop until reaching the rec.

I sat, panting, on a swing expecting at any moment to see hordes of policemen coming from three directions: North End, Loke Road and the railway footbridge. None appeared, so I ventured over the railway, along Kettlewell Lane, and hid under Highgate Bridge where you could be completely out of sight.

Had any of the people going past Boots recognised me? If so, they might tell Mr or Mrs Peckover. Worse, they might have told the policeman where I lived.

After some time I peered along Kettlewell Lane, saw it was clear, and returned to Mill Houses via the Saunders and allotments. As I opened the door Mrs Peckover exclaimed how late it was, and that I would have to hurry to be in time for afternoon school. They didn't know!

School was the next danger point. The errand boy knew I was a Londoner. What if the police brought him to school for an identity parade? However, the afternoon went off as usual. I did hear, at break time, that Boots had had stink bombs thrown in several days running, so it was hardly surprising they were getting fed up with them At the end of school I ventured out in the middle of a large group of others, keeping my head well down, and went home via The Walks to avoid the town.

I didn't go past Boots for a long time, making détours when necessary, but often had to slip into Cloughs, the fishing tackle shop, almost next door. When I did start going again I kept to the other side of the road, and looked in the other direction. I was sure that, one day, I would come face to face with the errand boy or manager but never did. I always hoped to meet the man who had helped me. When he had shouted: 'Hey, what's the big hurry?' it might have been with a Scottish accent, but I wasn't sure. I never saw him again either.

Not long after this incident I was sitting on the chaise-longue, reading. Mr Peckover was standing, looking down into the cul-de-sac when he suddenly darted forward and opened the window, knocking a brass ash-tray on to the floor in his haste. Mrs Peckover tut-tutted, but he took no notice and leant out

'Can I help you?' I was vaguely aware of a voice from below then Mr Peckover said: 'Yes! Here!'

He pulled his head back inside and, white-faced, looked towards me:

'There's a slopper!* Asking for you!'

Deciding there wasn't much point in rushing to the back window, jumping down into the garden and running off, I went downstairs. A burly policeman barred any escape through the gate. Already heads had appeared at many of the windows in Mill Houses. The policeman was frowning.

'Is your name Kenneth Regelous?'

I said reluctantly that it was.

'Will you call at the police station then? There's a reward for you.'

I gasped 'Reward!' loudly enough for everyone to hear from the windows. I guessed immediately what it was about. Some days previously I was walking past the bus stop at Townsend's Corner and noticed a multi-coloured, cloth bag on the pavement. I picked it up and showed it to people in the bus queue and shops, but nobody claimed it. Someone said it ought to be taken to the police station, so that was what I did eventually, pulling a school cap well down over my face before entering. There was a nasty moment when they asked for my name and address, but nobody treated me with suspicion.

When I went to collect the reward I again pulled my cap well down, but removed it before going out into the street again. Clutching a whole shilling piece, I had the pleasant feeling that my income was still rising faster than anybody else's.

*policeman

Country Activities

We hadn't been evacuated long when I found myself in a field near Gaywood where they were cutting corn. The others, all locals, had done it before, but it was a new experience for me and, although the picking up and carrying was hard work, I was sure it built up one's muscles. We broke off for lunch, and it was then I learnt what was to happen in the afternoon. We had been working from the outside of the field inwards, and there were lots of rabbits still in the island of uncut corn. When their refuge became too small they were going to rush out to be shot, or hit with sticks. After lunch, as the uncut area became smaller and smaller, there was rising excitement and the rush of rabbits was reckoned to be imminent. It was then I realised I couldn't bear to watch such slaughter, let alone help with it. I picked up my belongings and went off, never helping with the harvest again.

Another new experience was helping to drive cattle from the market, which was then between Lynn Museum and Norfolk Street. We used to arrive at the market and wait for cattle being driven away, then begin helping without bothering to ask if we were wanted. We were invariably useful because there were seldom enough men to control the animals. We already knew the area well, and were good at running ahead, guiding the animals along the correct route. Sometimes we left the market by Paradise Lane coming out into Norfolk Street, sometimes past the station or along London Road; it could be in almost any direction, and everything else would have to stop when we passed. Sometimes we went along Loke Road, so I knew exactly where cattle were likely to take the wrong turning. Some of the places we drove cattle to were several miles from Lynn, and it would have been impossible for the two or three men to have got them there without help. When we reached a destination the men would thank us and give us some coppers. Once I received sixpence.

Sometimes (but never when we were helping) cattle escaped when being driven along the Loke, and from the window we saw them running up and down the road. Many times we watched as they came charging down the cul-de-sac. Within seconds they had uprooted concrete posts, broken down fences and gates, and trampled over gardens. There was no stopping them rushing between the blocks at Mill Houses, crashing through fences and escaping over the dyke into the fields beyond. They left a trail of destruction in their wake, and it sometimes took the council men weeks to repair the damage, by which time another lot of cattle might have been along.

The cattle that ran amok along Loke Road sometimes came charging along the Long Pond. As soon as we heard bellows and shouts we knew what to expect: terrified animals would come at alarming speed along one or both sides of the pond, crashing through fences and hedges, getting into gardens and the allotments. At least once they broke through the kissing-gates, got on to the railway, and disappeared, some under Dodman's Bridge towards the station, and others towards North End and the docks.

One day a boy was fishing on the allotments side in the narrow gap between water and railings when three bullocks came running up from the Loke direction. The boy was so frightened that, instead of staying where he was, probably safe, he jumped over the rails right in front of the animals. Screaming, he ran before them towards the railway. Fortunately they turned left, smashing through a gate and ran up along the allotments.

Another time a young angler was fishing in front of the Tunmores' house when cattle came running up Harecroft Parade. He jumped into the water, waded level with the wire netting fence, and stood there. The animals stopped at the fence and charged back towards the Loke. The boy afterwards said that if the animals had got through the netting fence, he would have waded back to the side he'd been fishing from. I think all of us would have been prepared to jump in. Here, the cattle had the initiative, and it was very different from driving them. I often crouched down at the water's edge while cattle ran along the access road just above, and would have jumped in if they had come nearer. I was basically afraid of them even when helping to drive them, knowing they had only to turn round to knock someone flying, or tread on a foot to crush it.

We evacuees had never seen or even heard of samphire before, and it fascinated us. We saw it sold in shops and by men who came round with barrows, and we were sure we would make our fortunes if we collected some. After all, it was free! Several times we made long journeys to distant parts of the marshes, and struggled back for miles with a sackful each. It was much heavier than we had imagined, and we had to stop every hundred yards or so for a rest. Unfortunately there was very little demand for our samphire, and only twice did we manage to sell any - to friends of hosts. The first loads we brought back were mostly wasted, and I sold all my last sackful for only threepence.

Long Pond Games

Even before you got to the Long Pond you might hear noises that indicated what things were happening there apart from fishing. One kind of screech, for example, would tell you that someone (or, more likely, several people) had taken a leaf from a nearby hedge, made a hole in the middle, and was blowing it between thumbs. A different kind of screech meant that something similar had been done with reeds. Yet another noise revealed that someone had come to the pond with a supply of bones, which were being used as clappers. This happened quite often, and some children could play rapidly with both hands.

Most Long Pond games were accompanied by some kind of noise. Often we would make boats from reeds. You simply picked a reed, made a split about two-thirds of the way from the tip, and put the tip through the split, making a P-shape. You put the reed down on the surface and it would sail off at speed, the tip underwater acting as a stabiliser. These boats did tend to change direction every foot or so because of slight changes in the wind, but they would cross the pond quickly and, with a favourable wind, even travel the length of the pond. The sailing itself was silent, but the shouts that accompanied reed-boat races could be deafening.

You couldn't always tell from the voices what exactly was happening. It might be cricket or football played on the grass and access road between the Point and the Tunmores'. In these games half the time was spent trying to get the ball back from the pond, where it had been knocked in. The method of retrieval was to pelt the ball with stones, making them hit the water just the far side of the ball, so forcing it backwards. We were all pretty good at this through practice, yet it always surprised us just how successful it was. Even when the ball was nearly over the other side, and you might think it quicker to pelt it from there, or throw stones on the near side of the ball to drive it to the other bank, we would use the same 'driving backwards' method because it was so effective.

Stones were not the only missiles flying around there. We also had pea-shooters, usually made from a length of hollowed-out elder branch. The ammunition could be rice, split peas or anything else that would go through the barrel. My own favourite was a bike-pump handle with the washer end cut off. With that, and haws, I could blow twice the width of the pond. Using several haws at once I could usually hit a float out in the middle.

Another weapon was the catapult. Most of those seen at the Long Pond were made from a Y-shaped piece of branch, with bicycle or car inner tube for elastic. These were rather crude, but could propel quite heavy stones. You had to be careful to bring the whole thing downwards as you fired, or you were likely to hit your own hand. I had a favourite kind of catapult too. The handle was two clothes-pegs of the old 'dolly' kind, interlocked at about 60 degrees. The rest was made of elastic bands, looped together with a piece of thin material in the middle for holding the missile. Ammunition was a single lead shot. I always had ample ammunition because I used to buy the shot in large quantities to split and use as fishing weights. The large catapults could throw a stone a fair distance, but a lead shot from my small weapon went much further; I could reach the Point in the Long Pond from the Saunders. The other advantage of my catapult was its deadly accuracy; it rivalled the pea-shooter in this respect.

Archery was also practised at the pond, and we could find the wherewithal somewhere around. The bow could be made from almost any kind of supple branch or piece of cane. Any old piece of string or line would do. When I first saw Lynn boys shooting arrows I was amazed at the height and distance they could get. They could shoot them almost out of sight. Their secret was to have a very light arrow. Something as slight as the dead stalk of a nettle or dock would do, as long as it was strong enough to take the force of the send-off, and if it had a suitable weight at the point. This might be simply a piece of lead pinched on. My own favourite point was the end of a propelling pencil, which screwed on to the arrow. This lasted for a very long time until one day the arrow went further than intended, and I couldn't find it. With our simple equipment we could get arrows over the pylon lines.

Go-carting was a very noisy activity. Those who had pram or push-chair wheels could do it reasonably quietly, but the roller-bearing wheels were deafening, especially along pavements. Harecroft Parade and Harewood Parade access roads were ideal places for go-carts because of the lack of traffic there.

Rather quieter were the bike races. In the first part of the war we had to set off towards the Loke, go up to the railway, and come back the same way. But later, when the high fence at the Tunmores' gave way to a permanent gap, we could have races all the way round and as many times as we wished. Bike races tended to range further afield than go-carts, and would take in paths through the allotments, the Swan Laundry bridge, Raby Avenue and the Lily Pond.

There were often more bikes being ridden backwards than forwards round the pond. I didn't join in this activity much, my excuse being my late start at cycling and my large, heavy bike.

We also had tank racing! They were cotton-reel tanks, made from a slice of candle, a matchstick, an elastic band and a wooden cotton-reel with notches cut into the outside rims. The notches gripped on almost anything, and the tank would climb over grass, stones, piles of clothes, fishing tackle and most other things we put in its path. Young anglers often carried either a tank, or the material for making one in case there were tank races that day.

My own favourite Long Pond activity was wrestling. We would do this at any time of day, and all the year round. Everyone wrestled against everyone else. When it was a small boy against a bigger one, the latter had to throw the former within a given time or the smaller boy won. Wrestling took place where most of the other games did: on the grassy banks between the Point and the Tunmores'. I often wrestled against boys I had never seen before, and whom I never met again afterwards, but most wrestling was between boys who knew each other well. They were almost always good-natured contests, and very seldom resulted in lost tempers.

Long Pond cricket, mostly played along Harecroft Parade between numbers 1 and 4, wasn't limited to the cricket season; we sometimes played in mid-winter. Football also lasted the year round and was probably more popular than cricket. But the ball was usually the same, a tennis ball.

There were two activities that were strictly seasonal. The first was conkers. This started early in September with very unripe conkers, and went on well into October. There would often be contests going on all round the pond in the evenings, and the banks and access roads would be thick with shattered conkers and their cases. There were the usual claims of high-numbered conkers, like 50 or even 100, but most conkers broke only ten others at the most before breaking up themselves. And there were the usual processes claimed to harden conkers. The most common one was soaking in vinegar, but it didn't seem to work for me. Some Lynn boys seemed to have a secret method, and came along with conkers that were more like stones.

The other seasonal activity was concerned with peas - but not shooting them. For several weeks in the year there had only to be a shout of 'Peas!' and everyone would leave his rod and rush towards the Loke so as to waylay the pea lorry or tractor on its way to the factory.

We ran alongside the load, pulling out handfuls of both peas and haulm, letting some of them fall on to the road to be collected later.

Sometimes it was the anglers nearest to Loke Road who heard the tractor coming, and gave the shout: 'Peas!' In that case, if you were fishing at the other end of the pond, or in the Square, you didn't stand much chance of getting there in time. But you didn't always lose out if you were at the far end. The pea vehicles came from the Gaywood direction, and had to turn into Salter's Road at Highgate School, so they went past the other end of the allotments. Those fishing at the concrete end by the railway, or those sitting on the fences, could see the peas go past at the end of the allotments. Then the cry of 'Peas!' would come from the far end of the pond and everyone would have time to get to the road before the tractors - which had to go past Mill Houses, round the bend into Loke Road, and then do another hundred yards before getting as far as the pond. The drivers would then be met by even greater numbers of boys than usual, waiting on both sides of the Loke. If those drivers were ever surprised by the large numbers of us waiting, they didn't show it. Did they know how the message was passed on? They never slowed, speeded up or swerved, but just kept going at their steady rate with expressionless faces. The recreation ground was only about 100 yards further on, so by the time we had finished taking our peas, those from the rec were almost ready to take theirs. We sometimes got large amounts, but once we got back to our rods, and shared them round, they didn't last long, and we would then be on the look-out for the next load of peas.

There were nearly always children playing at the Long Pond, sometimes very young ones. One day a group of young children were playing hide-and-seek, and about twenty of them came running up from the Loke direction looking for somewhere to hide. At the far end of the pond, by the Loke railings, a boy was hiding his eyes and counting rapidly to a hundred. Neville's brother, still very young, was standing at his gate, and as the group of children came past he shouted:

'Come inter ours!'

There must have been about twenty children. They turned as one and piled through the Tunmores' gate, then through the front door. They had only just disappeared when the boy came running from the other end, having finished his counting. He must have taken a short cut or two with his counting because as he got level with the Tunmores' gate he stopped, amazed that there was already nobody visible. He looked all round without seeing the faces at the upstairs and downstairs windows. He went round the end of the pond, looked along the railway, and ventured a short way up the path towards the Swan Laundry bridge. Then the Tunmores' door burst open, and all the hiders ran, shrieking with delight to the Home point by the railings. Only a few minutes later another crowd was running up Harecroft Parade looking for somewhere to hide. As they reached number 1, Christopher beckoned:

'Come inter ours!'

A dozen sneering voices shouted:

'Not again!'

With a puzzled look on his face, Christopher stood and watched them run off to hide elsewhere.

It was hardly surprising that, with all these activities going on, there was often a shout of: 'Your float...!' followed by the name of the owner of the plunging rod and spinning reel. By the time we reached our rod, however, the fish had nearly always gone. We often vowed to keep by our rods and not become involved in anything else because we lost so many fish that way. But it was difficult to keep out of things at the Long Pond and, somehow, we always did get involved.

Comic Story

It was one of those go-cart days. I was fishing from the Boards, and every few minutes one of them went by, a boy in front, guiding, another one behind, doing the pushing and occasionally jumping on. Today's route was from the Tunmores', along the pavement to the Loke, then off left, probably around Harecroft Gardens, and back the same way. Most of the go-carts had roller-bearing wheels, and they were noisy. My mind went to the previous week's story in the *Adventure*. It had been about a go-cart race in which two heroes and two villains had competed. Everything depended on the result and, somehow, it was a question of life or death. The two heroes had been in the lead for most of the race, but the villains were catching up and, nearing the end, were beginning to overtake. It seemed that the heroes had pedalled themselves out and the villains had timed their effort perfectly. All seemed lost as the go-carts were level and the villains edged ahead. By chance the hero at the back happened to have some bellows and a supply of peas with him. He quickly loaded the bellows and, just as the villains were taking the lead, fired a deadly salvo of peas at the other driver. The villains' go-cart swerved and crashed, and the heroes won. All was saved.

As I watched a go-cart turn by the Roses' house I noticed Mr Pegg on the other side by the Lily Pond. He was talking to a boy, and pointing to the Long Pond side. I carried on fishing for a minute or two, then heard a voice behind me.

'Caught any?'

I turned round. It was the boy who had been talking to Mr Pegg. I noticed he had a split cane rod. Before I could answer, he went on:

'What are you fishing for? Nothing doing over there. Couldn't get a bite.'

The accent was definitely London, but I had never seen him around. Before I could answer his last question he put another:

'What sort of fish d'you get over this side?'

I decided to talk Norfolk.

'Caarp, rooch...'

Again he interrupted:

'You won't catch a lot with your bit of cane and that thick line, and your reel's miles too small!'

From a pocket he pulled out a piece of bait, and squeezed it on to his hook. He pulled line off his reel to the accompaniment of very loud clicking, and cast out with a splash. At that moment I had a bite and pulled out a two-ounce carp. Almost immediately the other boy reeled in. His bait had gone. He re-baited, and cast out again.

'Course, I'm used to fishing in proper, licensed places. I like catching specimen fish.'

I asked him what he had caught, but he didn't answer. He was watching

61

me pull in a roach, the same size as the small carp. He reeled in with a couple of flicks to the reel. His bait had gone again, so he re-baited and cast out. I had another bite, struck, and had another roach, slightly smaller than before. The other boy pulled in a yard nearer to where I was fishing. I continued to catch small carp and roach, and he was continually pulling in, having to re-bait, casting out and getting nearer and nearer to my float. He didn't get a bite.

'Funny! They must be sly biters here. They keep taking my bait without moving the float!'

His float was now only inches from mine. I was about to tell him about his bait, when a go-cart went by on the pavement behind. It had roller-bearing wheels, and made a deafening clatter. Before the noise had died away the boy said:

'I was roped in for a go-cart race in London a couple of weeks ago. Not that sort of thing, but a proper one with pedals. I was the only one strong enough, so they asked me to do it. The prize was a lot of money. We were in the lead most of the time, but then my co-driver cracked up. He was an eighteen-year-old, and the next strongest one they could find.'

'So whart happened?' I asked, still with a local accent.

'These others were just overtaking us and going to win, but the other boy saved the day.'

'How was thaat?'

'He'd brought along some old bellows and a lot of peas...'

I could hardly believe it, and forgot my accent.

'But that's amazing...!'

'He loaded up and shot a whole lot of peas right in the other driver's face.'

'What happened?'

'The others swerved, and crashed into a tree, and we won.'

'What a coincidence! I...'

'Thank goodness he had those peas and bellows. If he hadn't done that, the others would have won.'

'You mean he...?'

'Yes, I owed it all to him really.'

'Well, I've just...'

The other was modesty itself.

'If he hadn't done that, we'd have lost, and not got all that money for first prize. He saved the day.'

This time I managed to get a word in.

'That's amazing! Because I've just read a story like that!'

He looked puzzled.

'A story?'

'Yes, in the *Adventure!*'

62

Again he looked puzzled.

'*Adventure*? What's that?'

'It's a boy's magazine. And there was a story just like that last week!'

At that point I had a bite, and caught a good roach, over two ounces. I made as much of a show as possible getting it in. The other boy reeled in a baitless hook, put it in his bottom ring and walked off.

'Got to go now.'

He had been very convincing, and for a couple of days I saw it as a great coincidence. Then I began to doubt the story. He had been such a fluent talker that I hadn't managed to tell him about his bait. At least half the time it had flown off as he cast out. The rest of the time it had come off as it hit the water. If he had ever come back I would have told him. But he didn't.

Look! No Bait!

Jimmy Bone lived in a house in Townshend Terrace overlooking the Lily Pond. He was a young angler, but very reluctant to use the Long Pond cast. As a result he would often thrash the water a dozen times or more before being happy about his cast, by which time most of the fish had fled. But nobody ever complained because he was such a good-natured boy, and had no idea he was frightening the fish. One day I was fishing from the jutting-out fence on the allotments side when Jimmy came along and stopped to watch. My lump of bait was perched on top of one of the posts and, reaching out for it, I accidentally knocked it off. It fell into the water and sank out of sight. I said:

'Well, that's it! I had that bait just as I wanted it. Might as well pack up!'

Jimmy said:

'You don't have to. Haven't you Londoners heard about fishing without bait?'

'Yes, I think we've heard of nets.'

'No, no. I mean fishing with a gold hook.'

'Gold hook or not, you still need to put bait on it.'

Jimmy had his good-natured smile by now.

'No, you see the gold hook looks like something to eat, and the fish bite at it.'

I said: 'D'you think I'm simple old mate?'

'No, honest, Reg. Everyone's heard about it.'

'Where've you seen it then?'

'Well, a boy in the Lily Pond current the other week.'

'What did he catch?'

'Ah well, Reg, I didn't see him catch anything, but he said he'd caught a few.'

This was exciting news. Why hadn't I heard about it before? I hurriedly searched in my pockets, found a size sixteen gold hook and put it on in place of the bronze size fourteen I was using. I fished for some time, but didn't have the slightest nibble. I had been having bites all the time before, and it seemed obvious this wasn't working. I said:

'Don't believe it.'

'Try jerking it about a bit,' suggested Jimmy.

I jerked about for a few more minutes without a bite.

'The only thing I'm likely to get is a tiddler pike that thinks the hook's a tiny, this year's roach.'

I got down from the fence and prepared to go home. Jimmy said:

'You might as well have a try in the Lily Pond current.'

It sounded a fair idea. Perhaps the current made the hook move about in a way I couldn't. In the water that flowed in from under the Loke, the hook did move about promisingly. But I didn't have a bite although we stayed there for nearly an hour.

A day or two later when there was a group of us fishing at the Long Pond I happened to mention the subject. One boy said he had seen fish caught that way in the Lines current, and another young angler said he'd heard of it happening. A lot of us tried fishing with a gold hook for some weeks, on and off, but nobody claimed to have any success. One day Eppy knocked on the door at 23 Mill Houses. Mrs Peckover said:

'A young gentleman for you, Ken!'

Eppy was very excited, and breathless.

'Just heard, Reg! Someone's fishing at the Lines with a gold hook and been catching fish!'

As we rushed down the stairs I asked who it was, and what sort of fish they were catching.

'Don't know, Reg! Someone told me along the Loke so I just came up to get you!'

We ran all the way, taking the short cut through the allotments. As soon as we got through the first kissing-gate we could see there was nobody fishing at the Lines.

The gold hook story persisted for years. Several anglers claimed they had seen it happen, but nobody went as far as saying they had caught a fish without bait. A lot of anglers thought it was a story told to Londoners, but a lot of Lynn boys were convinced it was true.

There came a time, some years later, when catching fish with unbaited hooks was widespread and only too true. It was the practice of pike snatching. People went along the Gaywood River banks with treble hooks and a weight. They cast over any pike that was visible, hooking it anywhere: side, head, tail or stomach. It could hardly have happened before, when the water was deeper, more coloured and had a lot more vegetation for fish cover. But by that time the water level had gone down as a result of deep drainage, and pollution was beginning to have an effect. Soon you could go all the way from the Swan Laundry Bridge to the Stone Bridge in Wootton road without seeing a single pike.

Transferred

As 1940 wore on and I was still in the Rochelle Street school, it began to look as if I was there 'for the duration'. Then, without warning, it happened. In the middle of a term I was officially transferred. We never found out exactly what had brought the change about, but it was at least possible that taking the matter into my own hands had played a part. I was shown up the same two flights of stairs, this time by a girl who looked eighteen. Instead of turning right at the top, we turned left into a large classroom with a high ceiling and only about a dozen pupils. A lady was at a cupboard with a few pupils around her, and there was a buzz of conversation. A girl was giving out exercise books. It was rather different from previous schools I had known. The teacher came along and introduced herself as Miss Lathleen, and asked me where I would like to sit.

This was Mansford Street Central School, with which I'd been evacuated. The building was the old Technical School between St James' Boys' and the hospital. Between the school gate and the building entrance was a new-looking building, but very small - it must have consisted of only a couple of rooms. On the door was written: 'Education Office'. I wondered if these were the people responsible for my transfer. But I didn't think about this after the first day or two because my new school was such an interesting and happy place.

I never again saw any of the teachers who had been at the Rochelle Street Junior School, sharing the building next door with St James' Boys'. In one way this was a disappointment, because I would have liked to tell them how much nicer this school was than theirs. They must have gone elsewhere soon after I left because it wasn't long after my transfer that the Lynn boys were back on full-time schooling. A lot of evacuees must have left Lynn at that time.

A Bike

One day, quite out of the blue, Mr Peckover said: 'We'll have to see if we can't get you a bike.'

I had hardly ever thought of owning a bike. It had always seemed too expensive an item. But I could just about ride one, and what a difference it would make! I could get to all sorts of places there wasn't time to walk to; and the journey to or from school would be cut to five minutes, leaving more time for fishing.

A few weeks went by, and I feared the matter had been forgotten. But Mr Peckover brought it up again:

'I've got just about everything in the shed to make up a bike - except for a frame.'

This was a disappointment. Surely a frame was the most important thing of all. When I asked how we might get hold of one, Mr Peckover said:

'We'll have to pick one up somewhere. I'll keep my eyes open, and let me know if you see anything.'

If it was left to me I was sure I'd never have a bike. A frame wasn't the sort of thing we saw lying around except broken and rusty ones on rubbish heaps or, occasionally, in the water.

A week or two later I came out of a Saturday morning film show at the Majestic cinema. There wasn't time for fishing because, when I got back to Mill Houses, I'd be going out again to get the Saturday fish and chips for our dinner; but there were a few minutes to spare, and I decided to explore a derelict site next to the cinema. Right in the middle of the space, amongst some nettles, was a bicycle frame with mudguards. It didn't look very old because original red lines were still there, on forks and crossbar. It looked all right, but I knew it might be cracked. When Mr Peckover came in from work I told him what I'd found. He said it sounded promising, and I was to go and fetch it. I had hoped he would do that; a man carrying a frame would surely look less suspicious. Suppose a policeman stopped me and asked where the frame had come from?

But I did return to the site that afternoon, and stood for a while watching children playing. When nobody was looking I pulled the frame out of the nettles and quickly walked off, looking as casual as possible. Once past the post office and St James' Park I felt safer. There was hardly anybody about once I got past the station and went along Coburg Street and Wyatt Street. I went quickly along Kettlewell Lane, over the lines, through the allotments and along Salter's Road to Mill Houses.

Mr Peckover tapped the frame all over with a penny and pronounced it perfect. He soon started work on it, and it was quickly built up. Everything came from the bike shed: old cotter pins were filed down, and small nuts and bolts joined up three separate lengths of chain. For some time I used the bike only in Mr Peckover's company, but then I was a free agent. It was a wonderful feeling being able to have a look round at all the waters after the midday meal, and still get back to school in time afterwards.

My hosts used to walk their bikes from the shed, along the garden path, through the gate and round the block, then mount at the cul-de-sac. But I always seemed to be racing against the clock, and cycled along the garden path, negotiated the gate without getting off, pedalled past Ted Mindham's back door, round the corner of the block, then picked up speed over the kerb. My hosts warned me many times about the bump over that kerb, but I never could resist it. One day, going over it and landing on the road, I felt myself swinging up and down. To my horror I saw that the frame going down behind the front forks to the bottom bracket had snapped apart.

I expected my hosts to remind me about the warnings, but they didn't. I began walking to and from school, and imagined a broken frame was the end of it. But two days later Mr Peckover took my bike to a blacksmith friend who fitted a large bracket that bolted round the frame where it had broken, holding the two ends together. It was as good as ever for eighteen months - perhaps because I began going over the kerb more slowly.

Eeling with Sam Sutton

Although born and brought up in the country, Mr Peckover had never had anything to do with fishing. Then, one day he came fishing with me. The next day he went fishing himself - and caught something! After that, he never went fishing again. It came about through Sam Sutton, an eel fisherman.

We were at the table one day when Mr Peckover began talking about Old Sam Sutton whom he had met that day in town. The two of them always talked about horses because Sam had also worked with them most of his life. But by that time Sam had made the change to an internal combustion engine in the form of a taxi, and was often to be seen with it at Lynn station.

After some reminiscences Mr Peckover said: 'I told him you go a-fishin'.'

I asked if Sam Sutton knew the Long Pond. Mr Peckover shook his head.

'Long Pond be blowed! He go over the marshes somewhere. He catch eels, take them home, and he and his wife eat them.'

'The marshes? Where?'

'North Wootton direction.' Mr Peckover paused, and almost as an afterthought added: 'He said he'd take us eeling there on Sunday.'

I was still digesting this stunning news when Mrs Peckover added: 'We'll give you the 1/6d you still need for that rod, so you can use it on Sunday.'

This took a second or more to sink in, then I leapt up, fell backwards on to the chaise-longue and did kicks in the air. I had been saving for a 7/6d Millwards rod for some time. It had three joints, the bottom two red, and the top one yellow. It had brass ferrules and rod fittings, and was on sale in a shop in the High Street that some people called Cloughs, others called Gallyons, and yet others called Claytons. I thanked my hosts, and didn't stop smiling for a couple of hours.

I wasn't sure if Mr Peckover was coming with us, and when I asked, he said: 'Ah! I'll have a go. Old Sam's got lots of rods and tackle, and he'll fix me up.'

I bought the new rod, and it was then that Mr Peckover said he would take me to try it out at a place where he and Mrs Peckover had seen fish some years before. We cycled off that Saturday afternoon, past the station and South Gates to the River Nar, which we always called the Setch. There, I caught my largest roach so far. It was about six ounces. That was the first time Mr Peckover had ever seen a fish caught.

Sam Sutton arrived on foot early on Sunday morning, and we set off across the marshes. It was a long walk, and we finally arrived at a place I had never been to before: a wide stretch of water, quite choppy and looking deep. I tackled up feverishly and, before Sam had put their two rods together, had already caught an eel. Soon, Sam and I were catching eels regularly, but Mr Peckover wasn't getting anything at all. The wind blew our lines in unless we let line out to compensate, but he wasn't doing this, and I was kept busy casting out for him. Then I saw his float go right under, and shouted for him to strike. He didn't move, so I rushed over to him. He was fast asleep.

Mr Peckover could sleep anywhere, at any time. When he sat in his armchair in the evening, he would drop off even if the radio was on and people were talking. Sometimes he would fall asleep in the middle of a conversation. One night I woke up in the early hours and saw that the light was still on in the living room. He was sitting back in his chair, and I thought he might be ill. He had fallen asleep looking at a seed catalogue. In the first world war he had often slept sitting on horseback.

Now I was shaking him and looking for his rod. It wasn't there! Then I saw it a couple of yards out into the water, just below the surface, moving along slowly. Sam came up and cast his line over the rod, drawing it in. He handed it to Mr Peckover who reeled in, pulling out an eel only about a foot long. It was the smallest caught that day, and we never understood how it could have pulled the rod in. That was the only thing he caught, partly because he kept going to sleep. But we always reminded him that he had been fishing only once, and had caught something. Not everyone could boast that. Sam and I caught about 15 eels each.

It was late in the afternoon when we began to pack up. Sam decided we would get a bus home, so we set off towards North Wootton. We were sitting in a bus at South Wootton when a number of soldiers and policemen boarded the vehicle demanding to see everyone's identity card. Fortunately we all had ours. Identity cards were still being examined when a lady in front screamed, jumped up and ran off the bus shouting:

'Snake! Snake!'

It was an eel. We thought it must have escaped from Sam's bag.

Sam insisted on giving us a lot of his eels, so Mr Peckover and I arrived home with more than we had caught between us. I couldn't bear the thought

68

of all the eels dying so made several trips downstairs with an eel or two in a wet, canvas bag, and put them in the dike. The next day Mr Peckover noticed there were far fewer eels than the night before, and always maintained they had got under the floorboards. As he put it:

'Those jiggers get anywhere!'

Soon after that I learnt about the incredible journey every eel makes, as an elver, all the way from the Sargasso Sea. We saw them arriving every year in Lynn, and called them 'darning needles' or 'darnies'. It wasn't easy to spot them in the River Ouse, but they were easily visible in fresh water, swimming near the surface. Most of them came in at the Millfleet, under London Road into the Gaywood River. When they got to the sluice near Lynn station they climbed in their thousands up the wet, concrete sides, most of them getting washed down again. It was difficult to understand how any could get further upstream from there and we often spent hours, with nets and jars, collecting them and putting them upstream just the other side of St John's Walk. From there they went under the station and Highgate Bridge to the Saunders', the Long Pond, Lily Pond and Square. They even got into the electric light works pit and climbed, still in their thousands, up the stone base of the wide pipe bringing in the hot water. It seemed impossible that they could have got there via the Gaywood River because they would have to get up, against the current, from the Lines to the Long Pond, then into the Square, round the baffle walls and, most unlikely of all, up the steep pipe that brought the water from the Leccy Pit. The only other possible way was from the Saunders', with the water intake, and through the turbine cooling process, and that seemed just as unlikely.

But larger eels also get to where they are least expected. There was once a story in the local paper about a man who caught eels through a drain near Lynn Library. They were obviously in the tunnel that replaced the Fleet when it was filled in during the 1890s.

Once, when fishing in the Saunders' just at the end of Eastgate Street, I hooked what at first felt like the bottom. I was able to move the object slightly with my fine tackle, and gradually drew it in. It was an old bicycle tyre. When I had removed the hook I began to look around for somewhere to put the rubbish so that it wouldn't find its way back into the river again. Then there was a movement in the water at the bottom of the tyre. An eel about eighteen inches long was lying in it.

Mr Tunmore used to go 'holing' along the Gaywood River. Eels have two holes when they are in the mud, a larger and a smaller. The smaller hole is where the head is, and this is where Mr Tunmore dropped his bait. He usually gave his eels away to local people who couldn't afford to buy that delicacy.

We young anglers used to talk about 'eel nests' because there were several places where you could usually catch eels if you wanted to. One of these was in the Square, right in a corner where baffle wall met allotment wall. It was

69

the slowest-running part of The Square. You could fish as close as a foot or two from that corner, and never catch an eel, but you would usually catch one if you fished right in the corner itself. It was a difficult place to get to, however, and possible only from the far side of the other baffle wall.

Another 'eel nest' was a third of the way across the Long Pond right in front of the Billmans' gate. You could fish there for carp, and never get an eel. Or you could fish for eels a couple of feet away and never catch one. But if you fished for eels in the exact spot, you could usually get at least one.

One day Mr Hicks, the biology teacher, had been fishing unsuccessfully for tench in the Lily Pond. He finally came over to the Long Pond and, with his worm, unknowingly cast out into our 'eel's nest'. He hadn't been there long when he hooked something big. Passers-by stopped to watch, and several local residents came out including Mr Billman. They saw Mr Hicks catch an eel about three feet long. It was the largest eel any of them had ever seen, and I never saw or heard of a bigger one caught in the Long Pond.

Little 'uns and Big 'uns

There was a time every year - something like late spring to early summer - when, in the Long Pond at least, you could tell in advance that you were going to have a bite! The warning was dark vegetation and bubbles that came to the surface either in a large mass, or in a line ending at your float. We never really understood why this happened only at that time of year. The wise thing to do when you had this warning was grab your rod and be ready. When you had the bite it would usually be a vigorous one, and the float would go straight down, out of sight. When you struck you were at first convinced it was at least a two-pounder, perhaps more. Then you suspected it might be only a pound, then only half a pound. It nearly always turned out to be a four- to six-ounce carp which fought as strongly as a two- to three-pounder did the rest of the year. This raised an interesting problem.

A lot of young anglers gave up fishing by the time they were about fourteen years old but, if they didn't, there came a time when a decision had to be made between carrying on fishing for little 'uns, or going on to big 'uns; they didn't want to keep on catching the tiddlers that boys half their age were catching. So instead of fishing with a tiny piece of bait, near the side, these older boys needed to get right out into the middle of the pond amongst the big 'uns. To do this they needed to attach a reel to their cane, or get a proper rod with reel. Plenty of line was also essential, partly for getting out into the middle, and partly for playing large fish - which could take a lot of line out as they made off. They also needed to treat their line with Mucilin or a similar product to keep it dry so they could cast out and strike effectively. To be able to afford all these things most anglers needed to be earning money and, because the school-leaving age was then fourteen, that was when they could begin to afford the tackle needed for the big 'uns.

Christopher Tunmore and pike

The distinction between little 'uns and big 'uns was clear, yet subtle. If you fished with a small piece of bait, near the side, you were not likely to catch anything as big as three ounces. It would normally be well under two ounces. On the other hand, if you were fishing for big 'uns, you could get something as small as a four-ounce roach or carp. So it was generally accepted that a quarter-pound fish was a big 'un, and anything smaller wasn't. A different criterion supported this idea. With most tackle you could pull a three-ounce fish clear of the water. It was risky trying to do this with a four-ouncer, even if it wasn't struggling, so again four ounces seemed the natural dividing line. This explained why, when catching a three-ounce fish, many anglers wouldn't pull it out of the water, but got it to the side and used the landing net. It could then be counted as a big 'un.

So the problem posed by those hard-fighting, three- to four-ounce carp whose bite we could predict, was whether they could be counted as big 'uns, or whether they were really little 'uns.

There were one or two young anglers, but not many, who had proper rods and expensive tackle when they were very young, but these tended to carry on fishing for little 'uns until they were getting on for fourteen years of age. Neville Tunmore was an exception, and was fishing for big 'uns with all the proper tackle at nine years of age. His brother Christopher began even younger. But this was a family who lived on the very banks of the Long Pond.

Some young anglers changed from little 'uns to big 'uns overnight: one day with a cane, no reel, and fishing near the side, the next day with a proper rod, reel, and getting out into the middle as best they could. Other young anglers, myself included, took a long time to accomplish the change. I began thinking about big 'uns as soon as I got the small, bakelite reel on my cane, with a good length of Mr Peckover's snobbing twine. The problem was that this twine soaked up water like blotting paper, so I could cast with it only

71

once. After that, it had to be tiddlers again, or the Long Pond cast.

There was only one way of fishing for big 'uns without having to cast a long way. You could go to the railway end, climb out along one of the fences and 'put out' from there. With the fence length plus arm, rod and line, you could reach deep water. However, the fences were often taken up entirely by young anglers fishing for little 'uns, so I often had to wait for a place, and then fish patiently for big 'uns while the others were catching small fish all around me.

One morning I arrived to find the Harecroft Parade side already full up, so I took a place on the other side. I was fishing deep, hoping for a big 'un, but had caught only one little 'un, when a boy facing me, on the other fence, struck and met a lot of resistance. Not having a reel, he just had to hang on. I saw a look of panic on his face as he saw a big 'un thrashing the water. He tried to move past the other boys on the fence behind him, missed his hand hold, and fell backwards. I had a glimpse of him just before he hit the water, still completely dry and eyes tightly shut. Then two large waves rose from each side of him and he was underwater. His head came up just beside his cane, and half a dozen pairs of hands helped him as he scrambled out on hands and knees. He was lucky! He had just missed falling on to a submerged post that came up to within an inch of the surface. Someone had fished out his rod, but the big 'un was gone. The young angler sloshed off as fast as he could towards the Loke, followed by a friend carrying his rod. My float had been only a foot or two from him. Why, I wondered, did the big 'un take his bait rather than mine? He wasn't fishing for big 'uns, and I was! Seven or eight floats were now crowded where the boy had hooked his fish, all of them except one attached to canes without reels. The exception was mine.

As we carried on fishing I began thinking of the look of panic on the boy's face, and how for a fraction of a second he had been inches above the water, horizontal, with his eyes shut. I began to giggle. A boy beside me on the fence said:

'He's a-laughin'!'

I could contain my laughter no longer and, doubled up on the fence, could only utter things like:

'Panic...Eyes shut...horizontal...still dry...half wet for a fraction of a second...just missed the post.'

Eventually I had to throw my rod on to the bank, clamber off the fence, and sit on the grass holding my stomach. I was joined by several others, and not much more serious fishing was done for the rest of the morning.

Gradually, over a period of months, I did begin catching the occasional three-ounce roach. I longed for that magic quarter-pounder, but was pleased enough with the three-ouncers, and took some of them home. I put them in the copper outside, making sure they always had clean water from the dyke and plenty of food. Unfortunately all six or seven of them suddenly died one night. Mr Peckover suggested that I dig a trench in the garden, put the fish in that, and cover them over. It would be good for the soil also. Sadly, I dug the trench and removed the fish from the copper. It was then I saw they had all swollen slightly. It was a Saturday evening, so I left the fish in the trench uncovered until the next morning when Mr and Mrs Peckover's young nephew, Jack, was to come. When he arrived that Sunday morning I took him into the garden and pointed proudly to the fish.

'They're quarter-pounders!'

I don't think he ever knew what I meant.

It took a long time for the horror of those fish deaths to sink in. I loved fish, so how could I have done it? I had removed them from their home, and taken them to a place they must have found horrible. It was a terrible crime. My guilty conscience came out in a variety of ways.

The Long Pond was not *always* a hive of activity. Early in morning, late at night and in winter it was quiet. On school days it could also be quiet, and with fewer passers-by in mid-morning or mid-afternoon it was a silent and peaceful place. When there was little traffic and no trains you could imagine you were miles from anywhere. It was one of these quiet days when I was fishing from the concrete at the railway end, hoping to catch my first big 'un. I had a promising bite, and thought it might be my first quarter-pounder. It wasn't. I could see it was almost exactly three ounces. I was about to put it back, slightly disappointed, when I thought of the fish that had died in the copper. How could I possibly feel disappointment with this beautiful fish? It was a magnificent creature, living its natural life until I had caught it - only one of the dangers it had had to face. Being held out of water must be terrifying for it, and probably painful as well. At that moment I didn't care if I never caught a bigger fish. I didn't care if I never caught another fish at all. If only I could convey all this to the fish! If only I could convince fish that I was their friend, that they had nothing to fear from me, and that I loved them all! I kissed the fish on the mouth and put it back gently into the water.

I kissed fish many times in the hope of showing them I was their friend, and it wasn't only when there was nobody about. Others might be fishing nearby, people might be passing, or neighbours might be about, but I still managed it without being seen. I would look around carefully and if nobody was looking at that moment, I would quickly kiss the fish before putting it back. I don't know if any other Long Pond anglers felt the same, or did the same; I never asked them. And I never told anyone of my secret. But I know that many of them loved and respected the fish as much as I did. Nowadays, I understand, it is quite common practice to kiss fish before putting them back. But this may be only when they are specimen fish in some way. An angler from Somerset recently made a will leaving instructions that his ashes be mixed with his favourite ground bait, and thrown to bream in the swim where he usually fishes. More recently, one of the wartime Long Pond anglers told me he would like his ashes spread over the Long Pond:

'There'll still be one or two old carp who remember me!'

My old cane, even with the bakelite reel and a good length of cobbler's twine, never did catch a big 'un. One or two came very near the quarter-pound magic weight, but none quite reached it. The seven-and-sixpenny Millward's rod got me my first quarter-pounder in the Setch, the day before we went eeling with Sam Sutton.

It wasn't long after that day's eeling that I went fishing in the Square with the new rod. Nylon still hadn't arrived, so it was a useful place to fish in for big 'uns, no casting out being needed. Several of us were fishing, but I had chosen a spot right against the wall, near the tunnel entrance, in an eddy. I was fishing very fine, and had a bite that took the float right down. I struck, and was playing my first carp to qualify as a big 'un. Fortunately someone there had a landing net so I could land it in that difficult place with walls all around. It was a one-and-a-half pounder. I ran home with it, followed by several friends. Mrs Peckover said it was big enough to eat, so I left it with her. We ran back to the Square to find a crowd fishing exactly where I had caught my fish. I managed to get in amongst them, and into the eddy again. I had another bite, and caught another one-and-a-half-pound carp. Again I ran home with it, followed by friends, and Mrs Peckover said we could eat that too. Back at the Square there were even more young anglers fishing just where I had been. Again I squeezed in, got by the wall, and landed another one-and-a-half-pound carp. Yet again I rushed home with it. Mrs Peckover was now quite delighted because the three fish would make a full meal for the three of us - very useful in the days of wartime shortages.

I should have known I would have acute misgivings about taking those fish away. When I expressed these to Mr and Mrs Peckover they said that thousands of fish were eaten every day all over the world. But I could still remember the other fish I had been responsible for killing, and knew I couldn't do that any more. Every fish I ever caught after that went back where it came from.

The Long Pond Cast

When you fished for little 'uns there was no problem of casting out. You just 'put out' a distance rather less than the combined length of cane, line and arm. If you fished for big 'uns, you had to get out in the middle, but most of us couldn't do that by the conventional cast: pulling line off the reel, letting it lie on the bank, then throwing out. Before nylon came on to the market even the most expensive lines quickly got wet and wouldn't slip through the rod rings.

So most of us used the Long Pond cast. You laid your rod down, pointing up the bank, the butt about a yard from the edge. Having baited, you pulled line out, over the bank and across the road, and placed your baited hook carefully at the back of the pavement. You went back to your rod, picked it up, held it behind you for a moment, making sure no dogs, bikes, cars or people were coming between you and your bait, then whipped it over your head. Sometimes this was successful, and it went out into the middle of the pond. But things could go wrong. If you were too energetic you might leave your bait on the pavement, or see it go flying into gardens opposite. If you didn't swing strongly enough, your tackle might be only a foot or two out, or come draping over your shoulders. Anglers were known to hook themselves in clothing, hands, back of the neck or in the scalp. If they cast with too sideways a sweep they could hook other anglers.

Cracks in pavement or kerb could cause havoc. The slightest contact between either of these and your hook often meant a breakage - of hook itself, line or rod. I managed the Long Pond cast hundreds of times without breaking my cane but not long after getting the proper rod I snagged a bit of kerb and broke the top joint. Mr Peckover showed me how to get the wood out of the ferrule, and re-fit the top joint, and it happened so often that I could repair it there and then, on the bank. Fortunately, the break was always at the bottom of the top joint, so re-fitting wasn't difficult. But the top joint became shorter each time, until it was only a few inches and wouldn't fit into the ferrule. That meant buying a new top joint.

As often as not we helped each other when doing the Long Pond cast because it was quicker, and could be fitted in between passing dogs, pedestrians, cyclists and cars. But the helping part could be more dangerous than the casting. I always held other anglers' lines above the float in case they tried to cast out before I had let go. And it was wise to run well out of the way before giving the OK.

If you wanted to get right out into the middle, or a bit further, the back of the pavement wasn't far enough away, and the line would have to be taken through somebody's gate. You would then lay the tackle down on their path, sometimes with the bait on their doorstep. This meant even more obstacles: gateposts, hedges and fences, so there was even less margin for error. Sometimes residents came out of their door and nearly stepped on a piece of bait, or saw it disappearing pondwards. But it worked well and, on the whole, roads, pavements, front gardens and even the distances from houses to bank might have been designed with the Long Pond cast in mind.

The other method of casting at the Long Pond, before the advent of nylon, was to get someone to take line out, and go round to the other side. You could start at one end, on opposite sides, and move along, keeping level, until you reached where you wanted to fish. Your helper dropped your tackle in his side, and you reeled in until you were where you wanted to fish. This was less dangerous than the Long Pond cast, and you were not likely to break your top joint or other tackle. But it was hardly ever used. You had to get your line over other anglers and their rods as you moved along the banks, so this might explain why it didn't happen often. More likely, though, it wasn't considered a 'proper' cast.

Peter

During the war I must have taken a dog with me fishing hundreds of times. But it was always someone else's dog. The first dog I got to know was Peter, a sandy-coloured, smooth-haired mongrel. He belonged to old Ted Mindham who lived in the flat below us in Mill Houses. Ted Mindham was fond of Peter, and we often heard him talking to the dog of an evening. Ted was getting on in years, and I don't think Peter had ever been taken out for long walks before I arrived. He was affectionate, lively, easily frightened, a good runner and a magnificent jumper - he cleared most fences with ease. He loved being taken to roam over the marshes, but he hated water, and I never managed to get him to swim. When I was going out I'd knock on Ted Mindham's door and ask:

'Can Peter come out?'

Usually, before I had finished the question, Peter would have recognised my voice and already be pushing past Old Ted.

Sometimes Old Ted would say:

'He ent here.'

I'd then give a high-pitched call:

'Peterpeterpeterpeterpeter!'

Peter would arrive almost immediately from the back of Mill Houses or from the Loke Road direction.

When I took Peter to pond or river he would wag his tail all the way there, and even look interested when I began putting tackle together. But when he had been ignored for a while his tail would droop. He was utterly bored by fishing. He would stay around for half an hour, then wander off homewards. When I noticed him going I'd give him my call:

'Peterpeterpeterpeterpeter!'

He would stop, turn round, wag his tail and come running back. Then I would ask someone to keep an eye on my rod while I took him for a run through the allotments, along the Gaywood River and back by the Rope Walk. But sometimes he would slip away without my having noticed. When this happened I would pack up, go home and find him, and take him for a run over the marshes. Peter was the first dog I had ever been able to take for walks like this.

He was with me one day when I was fishing off the Boards. Nearby, in front of the Billmans', was a boy named Eppy who, seeing that a lot of people were walking or cycling past, asked:

'Hoi, Reg! Would you mind takin' my line back, please?'

Ken with Peter

I said: 'All right', and took his float, bait dangling, pulling out line to Mr Billman's fence. I was about to put it down when Eppy said:

'Can you take a bit more line out, Reg? I want to get right out in the middle!'

I opened the Billmans' front gate, followed by Peter, went into their front garden, laid Eppy's float on their path, and his hook on their doorstep.

'You'd better cast from a yard further along!' I shouted. 'Do you'll lose your hook on the gate! Hold you on a minute!'

I ran out of the front garden.

Eppy moved a yard towards the Point until exactly opposite the Billmans' gate, and stood poised for a moment, his rod tip nearly touching the road behind him. Then over came his rod with a swish.

There was a yelp, and Peter ran full pelt past me towards the Loke, Eppy's reel screaming as it could never have done before. For a couple of seconds he held on to his rod, arms outstretched and rigid. Then the rod flew out of his hands and hit the ground ten feet away. Peter reached the end of the pond, turned right along the Loke and, gathering speed, rushed homewards, pulling the line at right angles against the railings.

If there had been a couple of hundred yards of line on Eppy's reel, Peter might well have arrived at Mill Houses still pulling line out. But Eppy, like most of us, owned only about twenty yards. This soon came to a sudden end, and snapped. Peter continued his homeward flight followed by the tackle.

I made a dive for the disappearing line, and missed it. By the time I had got up and reached the road, Peter was fifty yards away, running fast.

I could already see what was going to happen. The poor dog would have to be taken to the vet to have the hook removed. Old Ted wouldn't be able to afford it, so Mr and Mrs Peckover would be saddled with an expense they could ill afford. Worst of all, I would be forbidden to take Peter out again. I knew I couldn't bear that, and would be reduced to taking him out secretly.

I did the only thing I could think of:

'Peterpeterpeterpeterpeter!'

Peter stopped, turned round, wagged his tail, and came trotting back. I grabbed his collar and began feeling for the hook. Perhaps I could get it out without Old Ted ever knowing! I glimpsed something pink and shiny at the end of the catgut as Eppy came running up. I groaned:

'It's pulled a lump of hair right off! You can see the skin underneath! It'll need stitches! Poor Peter!'

I cuddled the dog's head, and the tail-wagging accelerated. But then it seemed to me that the pink, shiny stuff moved. I groaned again:

'That's all comin' out!'

Eppy was daring to look closer.

'Wait you a minute! That aint innards! That's my night gobbler!'

He was right. But there was still the problem of getting Eppy's hook out. We could see the line twisted round Peter's neck and legs, and we began by disentangling his back legs. The dog was being surprisingly well-behaved. Eppy seemed to be better at this sort of thing than I was, and had taken charge. He had come to the line round Peter's neck, and looked hard.

'He haven't been hooked! He've been lassooed!'

Again Eppy was right. The line had gone round Peter's neck, tucked

78

itself into the hook's shank forming a running noose, and pulled tight. It was a simple matter to remove it all.

There followed a happy reunion of Eppy and line, just as there had been of Peter and me.

As I packed up my gear, Eppy threaded his line through the rod rings and back on to his reel. Then he cast out distinctly less ambitiously than on the previous occasion. Peter deserved a long run over his beloved marshes, and that's what he got.

I kept this story secret until long after both Old Ted Mindham and Peter had disappeared from Mill Houses.

Dead-Eye

It was the summer holiday and the afternoon was hot. A few of us were fishing from near the Point, not too optimistic about getting bites, and were spending much of the time launching reed boats from the other side. They took longer than usual to get across because there was very little wind. A boy rather older than us - he looked about thirteen - came up on a bike and stopped on the turning circle just behind us. Sitting on the saddle, with one foot on the ground, he nodded towards the water.

'Who's been making those boats?' We told him we had. He smiled. 'I can make proper boats. We've got a sea-going boat.'

We expressed interest, and asked a few questions which he was only too willing to answer. When asked if he went fishing he replied that he had been in for some competitions and won some prizes. I asked him what his main hobby was.

'I shoot rifles. I'm a marksman really.'

We asked him lots of questions about guns and bullets and shooting in general. He answered them all calmly and authoritatively without moving from his sitting position on the bike. His favourite expression seemed to be:

'Of course, I'm a crackshot.'

We were very impressed.

He was at the pond the following morning early, and didn't leave until we did at midday. He was already there when I returned in the afternoon, stayed until we left at about half past five, and came back in the evening. He talked all the time about shooting, and about how good he was, repeating all day:

'Of course, I'm a crackshot.'

By the third day he was known as 'Dead-Eye', and didn't seem to mind at all. In fact he seemed quite pleased about it. We tended to believe what he said because we knew nothing about shooting, and he was so confident and fluent.

One day someone brought an air rifle along to the pond, together with some small targets, and suggested Dead-Eye should show us how to shoot properly. We were all keen, and thought we could have a competition. Dead-Eye took the rifle with a disdainful look on his face, examined it carefully and handed it back, saying it was too crude a rifle for a crackshot like him, and would spoil his technique. I think we all believed him.

Another day we were having wrestling contests. Dead-Eye watched with interest from his sitting position on the bike. After a while I invited him to a wrestle. Warmly, he replied:

'I wouldn't like to hurt you, Reg!'

I explained that there was no need to hurt an opponent. It was only a question of getting him down, or throwing him.

'But I probably wouldn't realise I was hurting you, Reg, until it was too late.'

Again, I think we all believed him. Perhaps he was very strong, and couldn't help hurting people.

Dead-Eye was a Norfolk boy, and talked with a Norfolk accent, but wasn't from Lynn. He was in Lynn for a couple of weeks with some relatives.

On one occasion someone asked Dead-Eye what sort of targets they used in proper competitions. He thought for a minute, and then pointed to a telegraph pole by the bank on the other side of the pond.

'They're a bit like that pole over there.'

The questioner said: 'Poles? But that doesn't test whether you're too high or too low, does it?'

Dead-Eye put on a patient look, and went into one of his stories.

He went in for a British championship the previous year. He hadn't been allowed to enter before that, because he was so young. But because he was such a crackshot, he had been put in with all the men. The competition went on for a long time, with people being eliminated until, right at the end of the day, only the reigning British champion and himself were left. It was now between the two of them, and everything depended on the last shot. It was getting dark, and they were both exhausted, hardly able to raise their rifles. The champion had the first go, managed to raise his rifle, fired - and missed the pole! Dead-Eye, equally exhausted, just about managed to get his rifle up, fired - and just caught the side of the pole, slicing off a piece. He had won!

At various times Dead-Eye was also a champion angler, a champion boxer, and a champion racing cyclist. We tended to believe him although he hadn't demonstrated any prowess whatsoever. We hadn't even seen him cycle at much more than ten miles an hour, and he never went in for our bike races. He was with us all day and every day for two weeks, hardly ever getting off his bike. Then he disappeared. We half expected to see him the following summer, but he never came back. Perhaps his relatives weren't as interested in his stories as we were.

Stamps

Small, with two slim, short horns, almost straight, it looked like the head of the deer we used to feed in the enclosure at Victoria Park in the East End of London. Mounted on a shield shape, the head stared back at me with its friendly but sad eyes from high up at the back of the window. There were scores of other things around it: utensils, clothes, metal and wooden figures from every part of the world. But the forlorn head seemed to dominate them all.

I was on my way home from the cattle market, and had come across the window in Market Street, only a few feet from Railway Road. I stared at the head for a while, said a silent farewell to it, and resolved to come back as soon as possible.

The shop door, an antique in its own right, was on the corner of Market Street and Railway Road. Through it was visible some of the shop's interior. It, too, was full to overflowing with all kinds of objects. Just inside, was a rack with some kind of spear standing in it. Could it be a real spear? There was another window a few feet off to the right, in Railway Road, and from there I could see that it was definitely a genuine spear. It had a wooden shaft and a largish, metal tip which was nearly touching the low ceiling. Such a weapon might well have killed animals like the one in the other window; a sad thought – sadder than that people might have killed each other with it. Then I was aware of a figure at the back of the shop. An elderly man, pipe in mouth and hands held behind his back, was looking straight at me. I thought he couldn't be very pleased at having a boy's nose practically touching his window but, as if to show that wasn't the case, he half smiled, turned, and went out of sight through a door.

For the next few weeks I went past the antiques shop as often as possible, seeing many things of interest but, mostly, looking at the friendly animal and the spear. Small writing just above the door proclaimed the owner's name was Mr Emerson. The man whom I assumed to be Mr Emerson was usually there, pottering about, and although he must have been aware I was staring in, he took no notice of me. One day I was just about to move on to the window in Railway Road when I saw a notice, stuck on the inside of the door glass:

STAMPS BOUGHT AND SOLD

Why hadn't I seen it before? It looked old enough to have been there for years. I decided to put aside some of my pocket money every week and, the next day, wrote to my mother asking if she would bring my stamp album the next time she came on a visit.

Less than a fortnight later, armed with some coppers and a sixpence, I pushed open the door of the antiques shop. Even before the bell clanged loudly above my head I got the overpowering but pleasant smell of pipe tobacco. Mr Emerson appeared from the back, removing the pipe from his mouth.

'Good morning young man. What can I do for you?'

'You do sell foreign stamps, don't you?'

'Yes, we have a varied selection, and at all prices. But perhaps you'd like to look at this first.' He went over to the rack, removed the spear, and handed it to me. 'Interesting, isn't it?'

I could hardly say anything at first. It was quite heavy, and I touched the wooden shaft, then the metal tip.

'Is it a *real* spear? A native one?'

'Oh, perfectly genuine. Comes from South Africa, and it's pretty old. It's actually called an assegai.'

Mr Emerson went off, leaving me holding the weapon. I held it in various ways: ready to strike, two hands in front, in a carrying position, ready to throw. When I heard Mr Emerson returning I began examining it again. He took the spear, and handed me the deer's head.

'I think you're interested in animals too!'

The eyes seemed sadder than ever. I stroked the deer's head, feeling it was very like stroking a cat that had been run over. Mr Emerson said:

'Yes, it's a cruel business. One hopes the poor creature didn't suffer too much. By the way, it's a gazelle. It comes from Africa too, but from the north.'

He took the head from me.

'But you came for stamps! Let's see what we can find.'

He went off and came back with a large drawer which he put on a table. The drawer was divided up into sections, each crammed with stamps, some in packets and others loose. Some sections were marked with prices, and I was relieved to see there were some I could afford. There were many stamps I had never seen before. I was looking through a packet when Mr Emerson suddenly went off, leaving me alone with stamps still scattered all over the table. He returned with a lady. She was shorter than Mr Emerson, and smiling.

'So, you're a stamp collector? Do you have many?'

I told her I had hundreds, and that my mother was going to bring my album with her when she came to Lynn next. I chose some stamps and, as Mrs Emerson was putting them into a packet, Mr Emerson picked up another one from the table.

'You admired this one too, didn't you? We'll put it in with the others.'

I ran home and showed the stamps to Mr and Mrs Peckover, and told them how I had held the gazelle and assegai. They had never been into the shop themselves, and only just about knew it was there.

In London we had bought our foreign stamps in quite ordinary shops, and I had never been inside an antiques shop before. Only days before evacuation a cousin of mine, who also collected stamps, told me of a sweet shop less than fifty yards from home where they had recently begun to sell foreign stamps. He explained that some of their stamps were attached to cards by stamp hinges, and he went into detail about how you could buy one stamp and steal another. You pressed a thumb on a stamp at the left or right of the card, pulled it off and held it in your palm. If you held the card facing you, the shopkeeper could see nothing. You had to confine your choice to the right or left hand column so the shopkeeper couldn't see your thumbs moving.

We went into the shop and both asked for a card of stamps. Almost without looking, or choosing I slid off a stamp from the right, and got it into my palm. I handed the card back, and said I wanted to buy a stamp on the left. I put my hand into a pocket, dropped the stamp into it, and took out some money. The shopkeeper pointed to the place from where I had removed the stamp.

'There was a stamp here!'

My cousin began talking to him, but I screwed the stolen stamp into a ball, dropped it on to the floor, and fled. The cousin was a couple of years older than I, and a bit of a role model, and it came as rather a surprise that something he advised was a risky thing to do.

That sweet shop and Mr Emerson's were so different! I couldn't imagine trying to pinch a stamp here.

I became a regular visitor at the antiques shop, buying stamps, and becoming familiar with a lot of the antiques. There seemed to be a steady turnover, things disappearing and others taking their places. Mr Emerson knew a lot about stamps and often gave me some of their background. And he would always advise on the best stamps to buy.

There was another stamp collector among the evacuees at that time. His surname was James so, inevitably, he was known as Jammy. One day I was telling him about some upright Siamese oblongs I had bought from Mr Emerson, and asked if he had ever been in the old shop.

'No fear! An antiques shop's bound to be expensive.'

'But he's very cheap!'

Jammy looked doubtful. 'All right. How much did you pay for those Siamese oblongs then?' I told him. 'That proves it! I can get them cheaper than that, and you can see they're worth less than that from the stamp catalogue.'

Jammy knew a lot about stamps, but I was sure he wasn't right this time. I was sure Mr Emerson's prices were reasonable, and he often gave me an extra stamp - sometimes quite a good one. Some weeks later, Jammy was showing me some of his most valuable stamps.

'See that one? It's worth over £10.'

'Come off it! I've got that, and only paid a few pennies for it!'

Jammy shook his head, wisely. 'You haven't got the same thing. You may have the same stamp, but mine's overprinted.'

I resolved to look out for overprinted stamps at Mr Emerson's.

Jammy was billeted not far from Peck's Field, and often passed the Long Pond. One day I was fishing in the Lily Pond when he came walking past. I said:

'By the way, do you remember those Siamese oblongs I got from the antiques shop?'

'You were robbed!' He began walking away. I added:

'Well, they're both overprinted!'

Jammy stopped in his tracks. 'What? How?' I described the overprinting.

'Suffering catfish!' exclaimed Jammy. 'The old boy couldn't have known what they were worth!'

At one time I hadn't been to the antiques shop for several months, and the longer I left it, the more difficult it was to go back. But one day I was cycling past, with some spare money, so stopped, leant my bike against the wall, and went in.

As soon as Mr Emerson saw me he shouted: 'Well, look who's come! It's Kenneth!'

Mrs Emerson came bustling in from the back, smiling as usual. 'We thought you'd given up stamps.'

I made the excuse that I had been short of time, but would be coming more often again. Mrs Emerson's smile broadened, and she looked at her husband.

'We know where he's been, don't we?' She looked back at me. 'You've been spending all your time fishing, haven't you? We know you're interested in the fish themselves as well!'

Mr Emerson said: 'Come on! I'll show you some stamps with fish and fishermen. There's quite a lot of them, and I bet I've got some you haven't seen.'

Mansford Street Central

Changes were happening in my new school. There were fewer and fewer of us in those large classrooms, and the amount of room our belongings took up in the cloakroom was ridiculously small. There was some coming as well as going, but classes got smaller until the new term in September 1940 when the Blitz began. For the next year there were more new faces arriving, and class numbers increased.

The friendly and relaxed atmosphere at the school might have been the result of the small classes, but I think the main reason was the teachers themselves. They were all pleasant, and different in their teaching methods. At one extreme was Miss Butler (known as Moggy Butler). She took geography, and always had everything ready for every lesson: atlases, with page numbers written up on the blackboard together with references. Written and practical work were ready, with the right number of coloured pencils, outline maps, tracing paper and anything else needed. She had a series of mnemonics for each occasion. My favourite came when she was doing a lesson on Russian rivers; she got us all repeating:

'Ob, Yenisey, Lena.'

There was a Lena in the school at that time, and she had an admirer. Not surprisingly he became known as 'Ob'.

At the other extreme was Miss McDonald who took junior English. Her mind worked in unfathomable ways, and we grew to accept the change of topic from Defoe, to Shakespeare then to Milton in a few minutes.

Only a little less formal than Miss Butler was Mr Lewis, who took shorthand, typing and book keeping; linear subjects in which it was easily possible to measure your progress, especially the first two in which I was interested because I had the idea of going into journalism when I left school.

The teacher we had most, after the first year, was a Mr Bone. He took us for French and English Literature. Then, when the P.E. specialist left, he took us boys for P.E. and games. He gave the impression of never having prepared a lesson, but that could have been because he was so good at improvising when the need arose. We went through Shakespeare's *Julius Cæsar* steadily, but with long stops and discussions when some point of interest arose. Once, when he was stressing how clever and persuasive Mark Anthony's speech was, I questioned that view. Surely it was so obviously aimed at turning the crowd against Brutus that any fool would have seen through it! The discussion on this lasted for several lessons. When we had been at an earlier stage, he had asked a girl what 'Et tu, Brute?' meant. She was a lively clown of a girl, and promptly answered:

'Er! You brute!'

Some days before, Mr Bone had been explaining the difference between bathos and pathos, and he waited patiently for laughter to die down after the girl's remark. Then he said that this had been a much better example of bathos than he had been able to think of before.

In the fourth year a classmate and I found we had got ahead of the others in the French text-book, and we thought it would be fun to keep on going. We worked furiously and got a long way ahead of the rest. We finished off the tenses, and got as far as the present subjunctive. This didn't bother Mr Bone one bit. He let us go on, always marked our work, went over it separately with us, and made sure we took part in the oral work. Admittedly, the class was small, but it couldn't have been easy having us working separately, and it did mean a lot more marking for him.

The headmaster, Mr Roberts, was unsurprisingly known as 'Old Bob'. He took maths and mechanics with the seniors. For most maths, like logarithms and geometry, he was formality itself, went one step at a time and gave lots of exercises. But he also threw out all kinds of mathematical puzzles and logic problems to think about, and was never in a hurry to give us the solutions. I became interested in such things, looked a lot of them up and sometimes knew the puzzle's solution as soon as he gave it to us. But even in the early 1940s Mr Roberts was aware of the importance of topographical concepts, and was often stressing them. One day, to illustrate a point, he went out of the classroom, leaving one arm showing through the almost-closed door. He had gone out dressed normally, but returned with his waistcoat buttoned up over the top of his jacket.

It took me a long time to overcome the dislike of maths I had picked up in previous schools, and I went on for some years making no effort in the subject. Then, suddenly, just before some end-of-term exams, I decided it wasn't as difficult as all that and, if I wanted to, I could understand it all. So I made an effort at revision, and thought I had done quite well in the exam. Some days later we were having a geography lesson with Miss Butler, when a girl came in and said something to the teacher. At the end of the lesson, after Miss Butler had turned over the blackboard to display the homework, she announced that I had got 98% for the maths exams. The next time I met Mr Bone he shook my hand, saying:

'I wish I could get 98% for maths.' How different from my previous schools!

In my first year there was a married couple, Mr and Mrs Williams, on the staff. He took P.E. and she taught music. The music included one singing lesson a week in the hall. At the end of each singing lesson there was always time devoted to requests, and I don't think a lesson ever went by without someone asking for 'Riding Down from Bangor'. It is the story of a student in a train who is delighted to see a beautiful maiden enter the carriage. When the train comes out of a tunnel, an aged couple are disgusted to see an earring in the student's beard, and later on the student gets a smut in his eye. The village maiden 'turns herself about' and asks:

'May I, if you please sir, try to get it out?'

We always sang these last five words as loudly as we could, grinning and giggling. I shouted, grinned and giggled as much as anyone, yet it wasn't until years later that I realised the *sous-entendre*. I don't think many of the others could have been as naïve as I was.

Wartime was a period of scarcity, yet the school managed to obtain some unexpected things. One of them was 16mm films. Most of these were shown by Mr Hicks, the biology teacher. We saw laboratory experiments, speeded-up plant growth, agricultural processes, microscopic pictures of cells and insects, and many other things. They were black and white, and accompanied by the loud noise of whirring film, but we found it all fascinating, and it was a weekly treat. We also had films in French. These were well worn, and it wasn't easy to follow the dialogue first time, but when we had seen it two or three times we could follow it quite well.

We also had plastic! We had known about bakelite and perspex, but this was something new. It came in sheets, cylinders and rods of various sizes and thicknesses. With the aid of saws, files, sandpaper and lots of energy we fashioned useful things like table-lamps, inkstands, book-ends, condiment sets; almost anything. My own favourite product was a shark about a foot long that I made from transparent sheeting, and which stood up by means of the two pectoral fins and the tail.

We had a buff machine for the final polishing of the things we made, and this was not without its dangers. If you didn't hold on tightly to the object, or let the buff get a grip on an edge, your carefully-made product would be whipped from your hands, and propelled against the stone floor, then perhaps bounce up to hit the opposite wall, or even the ceiling. Everyone dived for cover as soon as there was the sound of plastic hitting the stone floor.

Another of the special things about the school was its large garden. It stretched from the road leading to the hospital, across to the far end of St James' school, and from the school hall, round the end of the hospital to the Gaywood River. The biology teacher, Mr Hicks, looked after all this, and gardening was another thing on the time-table. Mr Hicks somehow produced foolscap sheets on a wax machine with drawings and full instructions about growing all kinds of vegetables and fruit, and by the beginning of the fifth year we each had a large file covering just about everything needed for a garden and orchard. These were backed up by *Dig for Victory* and *Growmore* leaflets. We also had a fortnightly film on gardening and agriculture. Mr Hicks was enthusiastic, and worked extraordinarily hard. So did we, each having an area of garden which we dug and cultivated ourselves. One year I grew some celery, which meant frequent visits to the Gaywood River for water. One day I was pouring water between the rows with a watering can when something splashed out of the spout, and went quickly away along the trench. It was an eel about eighteen inches long that I must have caught when collecting water from the Gaywood River.

Once we were picking apples when Mr Hicks' ladder began slipping sideways, off the tree. He shouted a warning and somehow managed to drop twenty feet on to his feet. After that, we were careful always to tie our ladders.

In addition to all the biology and gardening he got through, Mr Hicks took the senior boys for technical drawing. I found this a fascinating subject, partly because of its connections with geometry. Geometry could be *used!* I was so interested that I paid the huge sum of elevenpence for a very professional-looking ruler with a metal edge. I got this from a shop on the corner of St James' Street and St James' Road, where the police station now stands.

As I was leaving school one day Mr Hicks came up behind me and asked if I had ever read a book called *Laikan (Laikan the Story of a Salmon* by Joseph Wentner, Rich and Cowan, 1934.) I had never heard of it but, when he said it was the life story of a salmon, and that the book was in Lynn Library, I lost no time in getting it out. It was a translation from the German, and I read it several times. The picture it painted of man, and his lack of feeling and respect for fish, was saddening, yet becoming familiar.

Mr Hicks was a small man with enormous ears. He rode a large bike with 28 by 1½ wheels and a wide carrier on the back for exercise books and other school work. He wore a trilby hat below which his ears stuck out. Not surprisingly, his nickname was 'Lugholes'. One day a few of us were going into the hall when one boy sang out, to the tune of the Westminster Chimes:

'Lugholes, lugholes...!'

There was a roar from behind. Mr Hicks had just come out of the main building to get to his classroom.

'Come here!'

We all laughed as the boy went into Mr Hicks' classroom because we knew he was going to get a couple of whacks on the bottom from Mr Hicks' 'bit of hazel' - which was, in fact, a hazel branch. I wondered why teachers were so touchy. Wouldn't it have been better to ignore the incident? For all the teacher knew, the boy might have been shouting the word for some other reason. But it was a common reaction, and corporal punishment was then a daily occurrence.

The piano that Mrs Williams used for our music lessons was the only one in the school, and it must have come in for some rough treatment because at an assembly one morning Mr Roberts said that nobody was allowed to use it without permission, and that permission could come only from him.

A day or two later, making sure nobody was about, I slipped into the hall and sat down at the piano. The Warsaw Concerto, from the film *Dangerous Moonlight*, was very popular at the time, and I had learnt to play it with two fingers. I had got through it twice when Mr Roberts came striding through the door.

'What are you doing?'

'I'm playing the piano.'

'Really? And what are you playing?'

'The Warsaw Concerto.'

'Let's hear it then!'

Concentrating hard I gave my two-finger rendering. As the last note died away I looked up, expecting to see fury on Old Bob's face. He didn't look furious, but got up, and said: 'Quite good!'

He went off without another word. It had, actually, been my best performance of the Warsaw Concerto.

On the whole we had a lot of P.E. and sport, which was very much to my liking. The favourite game was soccer, which we played at every opportunity with a tennis ball in the playground. We also had a proper game every week on The Walks, where we would arrive, change under the trees, pick sides and play for as long as possible with a teacher urging us to pass instead of trying to dribble the length of the field. We played whatever the weather, sometimes having to change into clothes that had got wet in the rain as we played. There was no shelter except for the trees. Only once do I remember this soccer routine being interrupted, and that was when a bomb fell on one of the pitches we used. There was a huge crater. But we missed only one week, although it was some time before the crater was filled in.

Once a week we had swimming in the outdoor pool on The Walks, near the bandstand. This went on all the year round with no cancellations for bad weather. In winter we often broke the ice before going in and, when getting out, our bodies gave off clouds of vapour.

Soon after I started at the school Mr Roberts saw me playing tennis with my age group. He said: 'You should be playing with the seniors!'

To my delight that meant I had tennis twice a week instead of once. We used the grass tennis courts not far from St John's Church. On one side was a high wall separating the courts from Lynn station. The head was keen on tennis, and coached us as much as he could in French because he was keen on that, too.

A favourite playground game of our own was shoulder-charging. The field of play was the semi-circle of a netball court in which we hopped on one foot, trying to shoulder-charge an opponent outside the semi-circle. It was as much a case of dodging and weaving as of charging. After a few minutes of that your hopping leg was a bit weary!

Our sport and games were almost entirely informal. When we played soccer on The Walks we simply picked sides on the spot. Only once did we get a soccer match against another school, and that was Gaywood Park. As with the first Lynn *v.* London match some years before, we had a problem finding eleven players, and fielded some very young boys. The Gaywood Park boys were all good, and one of them, a boy called Benefer, whom I knew slightly, not only got his head to the ball frequently but also, to our surprise, managed to find one of his team when he did so. We lost heavily.

Occasionally Mr Bone organised a cycle ride on a Saturday. Once we went to Hunstanton, going via Fakenham where, because it was so hot, I spent all the money I had (2d) on some sticks of rhubarb to quench my thirst. At that time Hunstanton was full of RAF personnel, and most of them seemed to spend all day in the swimming pool. They all looked very fit, but probably quite a lot of them didn't survive the war.

Most of the teachers cycled to school, and there were two very keen cyclists: Miss Lathleen and Miss Tring. They both had brand new Claud Butler bikes which they kept immaculately clean. One day they announced a cycling week-end to the King's Cliffe youth hostel, the other side of Peterborough. I imagined there would be lots of takers for such an exciting trip, but only one other pupil was interested: a girl about two years older than I was, named Louise Peasgood.

As we were cycling out, near Wisbech, Miss Lathleen looked around and said: 'I suppose this is fenland at its best!'

It was indeed a fascinating area. There were hardly any hedges, and few trees, but there was a lot of water. Every field was surrounded by a ditch or dike. I was soon stopping every few minutes to look at the water to see what fish might be there. There were sticklebacks, but also roach and small pike, and signs of tench. What with the fish, duck, geese, water voles and other wildlife, the other three were also excited, and quite willing to make frequent stops and look around.The water level was high, and I was sorry we weren't staying in the fens for the week-end.

Around midday Louise and I, having explored a ditch, became separated from the two teachers, and got completely lost. All the signposts had of course been removed, so we had to guess which turns to make. There was nobody else about, and no cars, but we did eventually meet an RAF man, cycling in the opposite direction. It was a heat wave, yet he was dressed in full RAF uniform, complete with cap. I had never seen anyone sweating as much. He took pains to put us on the right road, and we suddenly came across the two teachers sitting by a crossroads eating their sandwiches.

King's Cliffe hostel was occupied mainly by conscientious objectors - about whom one heard only unfavourable reports at that time. But all four of us got on very well with them, and were invited to take part in a play they were putting on that week-end. It was an unforgettable experience, and I was determined to go back there as soon as possible. I did, but not until 1946 when on a hostelling tour to Scotland. Louise intended to go into teaching, and I have often wondered if she did.

Another activity was ballroom dancing. We danced to records (78s) at lunch times, after school and sometimes in school time. I was once tempted to go to one of the 'proper' dances on an upstairs floor in the Co-op building in Norfolk Street, but was a bit out of my depth, and never went there again.

One Saturday morning Mr Hicks organised an angling contest on the banks of the Gaywood River in the school grounds, and seven or eight of us took part. Mr Hicks caught a very nice roach of about 6 ounces. Les Marriot had an eel, and I caught a gudgeon. The others didn't catch anything. The eel was something over 3 ounces, and my gudgeon only slightly less. It was the largest gudgeon I had ever seen, and couldn't have been far from a British record, but Les won the contest with his eel. Les Marriot was one of the few evacuees to take up fishing while in Lynn - which wasn't long because he was soon of leaving age. Not long after our fishing competition he was fishing in the Long Pond with a chip and, reeling in, was surprised to feel something grab his bait. A crowd gathered round as he played and landed a one-and-a-half-pound pike. As he went off with it he shouted at the top of his voice:

'I only got it on chip!'

He took the pike along to Lynn Museum and asked them if they would like to stuff it and put it in a glass case. They politely refused, having already several twenty to thirty-pounders. But Les did get his name in the local paper as a result.

Glorious Mud

In London the nearest grass we could walk on was at Victoria Park, about a mile away, and we sometimes went for a picnic there just for the pleasure of sitting on it and walking over it.

In Lynn there was grass everywhere. Just at the back of Mill Houses there were whole fields of it. Even in the town there was grass in front of the school, in the Walks and St James' Park. It was all along the Gaywood River and around the Long Pond. Mr Peckover had to work hard to stop it growing in the garden and even along the paths.

With the grass there was mud, and that was even better. We had hardly known mud before, yet here it was all over the place: along ditches and dikes, with the grass round the Long Pond and in the garden. Over the marshes there was sometimes mud for as far as you could see. And the slimy, squelchy mud of the Fisher Fleet and River Ouse was really something special.

Often, when Mr Peckover came home from work, he would ask:

'Hev you been a-mud plumpin' agen?'

When I first explained how we didn't have mud in London, and how marvellous it could be, Mr and Mrs Peckover were surprised. They had always had too much of it, but when they realised how much we appreciated it they soon began talking about 'Good old Norfolk mud'.

Walking over the marshes one day a group of us came across a cluster of fresh mole-hills. We were soon picking the soil up, squeezing it into balls and throwing them at each other.

We had discovered mud-balls!

From then on, mud-ball fights were a favourite activity. Sometimes we stood only a few yards apart and simply pelted each other. Sometimes we lobbed them at each other over an embankment. Sometimes we stalked each other.

We made mud-balls of different sizes depending on the state of the mud, distance and wind. The most important factor was usually the wind. If you could keep upwind of your opponents you could have them within range, and they couldn't reach you. But there was no point in being too far away because your opponents then had time to see your mud-balls coming and dodge them.

Usually we used a mud-ball as soon as it was made; but sometimes we carried them around. The longer you held and shaped a mud-ball, the more shiny and round it became. If it didn't crack you were soon reluctant to throw it away. I often carried one around for a long time, eventually taking it home and putting it in the garden.

A few of us were on the banks of Clark's Dyke one day between the bridge-that-went-nowhere and the end of Loke Road. There was such a strong wind blowing that we had given up mud battles and were seeing who could throw furthest. We threw mud-balls with the wind, across Clark's Dyke, further than we had ever done before. Then we saw a back garden with washing hanging out, blowing almost horizontal. After one or two experiments, throwing high to take full advantage of the wind, one of us hit a sheet. Soon we were hitting the washing again and again; when we eventually ran off there was more mud colour than white showing on the washing.

It must have been two years later that a few of us were returning from the marshes. Although I had more Lynn friends than London ones by then, it so happened that we were all evacuees. Suddenly we heard shouts from behind. A dozen or more boys were running towards us.

'Bloody Londoners! We'll murder you!'

The obvious thing to do was break into a run, keeping a safe distance between us and them. We were all fairly good runners, only half a mile from home, and confident we could keep far enough in front to avoid trouble. We began running steadily, but realised one of us was missing. Mo Miller was still walking. We urged him to run with us, but he refused, saying he wasn't afraid of them. He was a tall, strong boy, but wouldn't have stood much chance against a dozen of them, so we stopped running and were soon caught up by the Lynn boys. We were harassed although the others, some of whom I knew fairly well, wouldn't go as far as actually starting a fight. But when we got to Turbus Road, just opposite Southgate's shop, they were on home ground and fights started. I found myself grappling with one boy and, seeing another coming up, I managed to push the first one into a hedge and turned to face the other. This boy snarled:

'You're the one who threw mud all over my mother's washing!'

I feigned surprise. Surely he couldn't know this after a couple of years.

'What are you talking about?'

'Don't bother denying it. Everyone knows curly top!'

At that moment a couple of men who were cycling past dismounted and pushed in amongst us.

'Come on! What's all this about? You ought to know better at your ages!'

We hurried off, happy to leave it there. I think the Lynn boys were of the same opinion - except perhaps for the boy whose mother's washing we had ruined all that time ago.

Scrumping

To us, arriving in Lynn, it seemed that every other tree bore fruit. In Mr Peckover's allotment there were several apple trees, three pear trees and three old plum trees. Apple trees overhung many roads and pavements, and a lot of fruit rotted on the ground. We ate fruit, especially apples, continually. Tummy aches didn't deter us. Some fruit trees were in public places, but even these were not safe from us. There were two pear trees near the river in Kettlewell Lane, but the pears never had a chance of ripening because we picked them, and ate them, when they were the size of a thumbnail. We once discovered an almond tree in Tower Gardens, and left with pocketfuls of almonds. When I told Mrs Peckover what we had found, she told me not to do it again because it was a memorial garden, and picking fruit there was wicked.

But there were real orchards! The largest was Taylor's Orchard in Tennyson Avenue. In its hedge, along the pavement, there were two holes that were never blocked up. There were several methods of scrumping. You could look through one of the holes to make sure nobody was about, crawl through, grab your fruit and crawl back onto the pavement in Tennyson Avenue. You could also gain entry over a gate in Gaywood Road near the Woolpack, but that was risky because if you had been spotted from a nearby window you might be apprehended on the way back. To avoid that risk you could climb the gate, then rush right through the orchard, and emerge with your fruit through one of the gaps in Tennyson Avenue. The first time I did this I was halfway through the orchard when I realised the gaps might have been blocked, so I could be trapped. That was a bad moment. You could do it the opposite way round, entering at Tennyson Avenue, and get out at Gaywood Road. I never tried that. Of course, the main attraction was the fruit, but as far as I was concerned, a close second was the marvellous smell in an orchard.

For young anglers of the Long Pond area the main source of illicit fruit was an orchard adjoining the Lines railway bridge. The owner was Mr Petts, known as Piblo Petts. He was a spare, long-faced man who always wore a cap; we never knew what he looked like without it on. He defended his orchard remorselessly. His hedge was criss-crossed with barbed wire, and any weak place that appeared was immediately repaired. It should have been easy to get into the orchard between the end of Mr Petts' hedge and the river because the wide pipe, bringing water from the Long Pond, gave a firm foothold. But Mr Petts had erected defences of barbed wire and corrugated iron sheets that projected well out over the water. The only way in or out of his orchard was through a hawthorn hedge a few feet from the river, where the barbed wire was pushed up or down so frequently that even he couldn't always keep it scrumper-proof.

By the autumn of 1940 I was often fishing at the Lines, and Mr Petts would growl at me from his land, accusing me of stealing his apples. Actually, I had very seldom set foot in his orchard, and never alone. It was too difficult to get into, and certainly no place to have to get out of quickly. And by that time I didn't need to go there. Several of Mr Petts' trees overhung the river just upstream of the bridge and one day, casting out too high, I got snagged in them. Not wanting to lose my tackle I removed shoes and socks and waded out far enough to reach the line, pull a branch in with it, and rescue everything. During this operation several apples fell off into the water. They were carried to the opposite bank by water gushing from the Long Pond pipe, then floated downstream. I rushed to the other side of the bridge, and was in time to lean over and pick two of them out. So after that I used a handline with a stone loosely tied to the end. I threw it into the trees upstream, gave a few tugs to dislodge the fruit which floated downstream and was diverted to the far bank by the current from the pipe. It always reached the bridge at the same place - a couple of feet from the bank. And there was always time to pull the line out of Mr Petts' trees before collecting the fruit. If the line seemed to be stuck, I had only to give an extra-strong tug, and the stone would fall off into the water, leaving the line free. I sometimes also got pears this way, but they were less buoyant than apples, and had to be grabbed or netted below the surface. Plums sank too quickly to be a possibility. I don't think Mr Petts ever found out. Perhaps he wouldn't have minded because he never bothered collecting fruit that overhung the water.

I was fishing upstream from the bridge one day when a movement on the other side of the orchard caught my eye. Mr Petts had just flitted from behind one trunk, and was now hiding behind another. I pretended to look down at the river, but could see his cap sticking out. Then he went nimbly behind another tree, then another, getting nearer all the time. He spied on me for a good half-hour before starting to stroll about as if he had just arrived. After that, when he got into his orchard, if he saw me fishing he would go through the same procedure. So whenever I did venture into his domain I had to be very careful.

Another time, quite by accident, I happened to see him spying on me from behind a pillar on Dodman's Bridge. Although he was then only fifty yards away, he had a walk of something like three hundred yards to get to his orchard because he had to go along to Salter's Road, then to the Swan Laundry Bridge, then along the footpath to the allotments. Once, when I saw him looking from the bridge, I got up and walked to the wired gap of his orchard, and made as if to get in. His cap disappeared immediately. I saw him arrive through his door, breathless, by which time I was sitting on the bridge busy fishing. Sometimes, when fruit was about, I would take an apple with me when fishing the Lines, and if I saw Mr Petts spying I would take it out and start munching at it. My ambition was to have an apple with me when he peeped from Dodman's Bridge, so I could pretend to go scrumping and, when he arrived breathless, be eating my apple. I never did manage it.

I knew lots of Lynn boys who raided that orchard a lot more than I did, but years after I had stopped scrumping, Mr Petts was still convinced I was his arch-scrumper. One day I was walking with Mr Bone, one of our teachers, along Blackfriars Road towards Littleport Street. We were opposite St James' Girls' School when Mr Petts appeared from the other direction pushing a large wheelbarrow piled high with fruit. He was on his way to the station with it. He looked over towards me and shouted: 'Here's a few you didn't get!'

Mr Bone, whose garden was on the opposite bank to Mr Petts' orchard, and adjoined the Lines Bridge, said: 'He seems to know you, Ken.'

Mr Petts had looked as angry as ever. I never saw him smile - but perhaps he did when I wasn't around.

I am sure Mr Petts went to his grave convinced I had robbed him of much more fruit than I ever did. When he did die, he was a rich man. Strangely, some years after his death, I often went into the orchard and fished from the banks there. Mr Tunmore, whose allotment was alongside, was acquainted with the new owner, and was allowed to fish there and invite any of his friends. It was a wonderful place to fish from, but I sometimes felt I wasn't alone, and half expected to see Piblo Petts flitting from tree to tree.

Wartime Lynn

We evacuees were only one part of the evidence in Lynn that there was a war on. For some time hardly anyone went about without carrying a gas mask. Usually they were in their original cardboard boxes which was protected by waterproof material, but some people had metal, cylindrical containers that were completely waterproof. I would have liked one of those, and often wondered why they were not more popular than they were.

Right at the start of the war there was a brick and concrete machine gun post only 30 yards from Mill Houses, and visible from our windows. This remained long after the war. A huge air raid shelter was built along the Kettlewell Lane Gardens, and that too remained until long after the war.

Wellesley Barracks soon spilled over into neighbouring parts of 'Lower Canada', as more buildings were acquired for housing soldiers. As we walked to school we had to pick our way over pavements covered with drying webbing and polished boots, and duck under washing or newly-pressed uniforms that hung between windows and makeshift posts in the gutter.

Marching soldiers were a common sight, and attracted large numbers of boys who kept in step alongside them. Once a Scottish military band marched around the town. All the soldiers wore kilts, and one drummer had a knife stuck in his sock. We all longed to have a real dagger like that! A lot of us followed that band for nearly two hours.

95

A favourite pastime was going around the town looking for soldiers and asking: 'Got any buttons or badges please, Mister?'

The patience of those soldiers was remarkable, even allowing for the wartime spirit prevalent then. They would stop and search through pockets for anything they could find, and were disappointed if they couldn't give us something. As often as not they did, even if it was only a general service button. They often removed a shoulder badge and gave it to us, and I once saw a soldier take out his penknife and cut off a button so he could give it away. Once, by the Pilot cinema, I saw a soldier wearing a peaked cap, carrying a large suitcase in one hand and a bulging kitbag in the other. I ran up to him.

'Got any buttons or badges please, Mister?'

He was a short man, and when he leant down to rest his luggage on the pavement his head wasn't much higher than mine.

'Therzwononmekeptekit.' At first I thought he was telling me to run away, but he nodded his head in a friendly way.

'Therzwononmekeptekit.'

He was saying: 'There's one on my cap, take it.'

I reached up and lifted the badge off his cap, thanking him, hardly believing I could be so lucky. He picked up his luggage and walked off past the cinema, badgeless. I hope he didn't meet any military policemen. It was a brand new, Royal Artillery badge, carefully bent to fit the curve of a peaked cap.

There were also lots of American servicemen in the area, and as they walked around Lynn they had to run the gauntlet of hordes of children shouting: 'Got any gum, chum?'

I was never interested in chewing gum myself, but often saw Americans tossing packets of it at groups of children. They must often have been carrying a lot about with them.

Neville's sister had a boyfriend in the American air force who, knowing Neville was interested in fishing, gave him a fishing line from the lifecraft of a Flying Fortress. It was the best line Neville ever had, and it lasted him years. He never heard that it was needed for survival, but he would probably never have known if it had.

A lot of boys became interested in aircraft-spotting, bought books on the subject and became remarkably knowledgeable. That never interested me, but I did have a craze for digging trenches. Only days before evacuation, men had begun digging trenches in a small park not far from where we lived, and I was among hundreds of boys who went along. We helped them to fit up large boards with 6-inch nails - many of which finished up in our pockets. This whetted my appetite for trench-digging, and Mr Peckover's allotment was at one time covered with a network of trenches 5 to 6 feet deep. I think his vegetable output went down drastically.

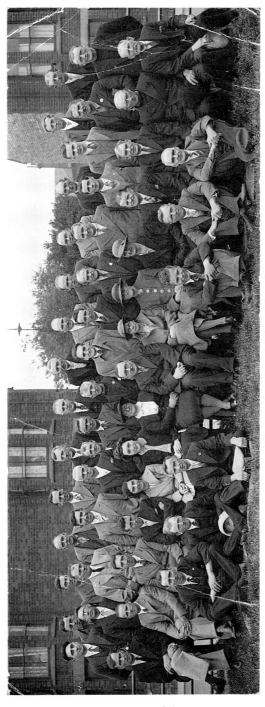

The Loke Road Fire Watchers

This photograph was taken on the Loke Road recreation ground next to the ARP post. Tom Mitchley stands in the back row third from the right. M.A.Knights ('Knights') is seated on the far right. On the grass, third from the right, is Tommy ("Tufty') Miller, an evacuee and a pupil at Mansford Street Central. Seated in the centre amongst the ladies is Mr ('Hungry') Fisher. On the grass, third from the left, is Mr Pegg, and seated third from the left is Wilfred Peckover.

There was a much-discussed interest of another kind when a man in Harewood Drive developed a passion for Vera Lynn, losing interest in his wife and family. He had never seen Vera Lynn, only heard her voice.

When there was an air raid warning at night we sometimes got up and chatted to neighbours at Mill Houses. Lots of people claimed they could tell the difference between allied and German aircraft, and it often seemed they were right. We would hear the crunch of bombs when standing around at night, not knowing where they were landing. But by the next morning, everyone knew where the bombs had fallen.

There was an air raid warning one night, and Mr Peckover was sure the planes he could hear were German, so he woke me up. We were looking out of the back bedroom window when we suddenly saw flames and sparks shooting upwards not far off. Mr Peckover exclaimed:

'They're fire bombs on the grammar school!'

He was right. They were bouncing on the roof and the tower of the building, and it was a spectacular sight. Prompt action avoided major damage.

During another night alert I was looking from my bedroom window along Loke Road when there was the noise of a low-flying aircraft, and tracers went up from the docks area. These had hardly come into sight when other tracers from an aircraft I couldn't see came down towards them at exactly the same angle.

In the summer of 1942 one of Mrs Peckover's sisters, Flo, was spending the day with us. Her husband was in the RAF, and stationed near Lynn, so they were able to see each other. We were all in the dining room when there came the noise of a low aeroplane approaching fast. We rushed to the window to see the plane and four wobbling objects just below it. Flo exclaimed:

'They're bombs, look!'

Everyone else rushed to the far side of the room, but I had opened the window and was still trying to shut it again when it was pulled from my hands by the blast. One of those bombs landed on the Eagle Hotel in Norfolk Street killing 42 people, and injuring a lot of others. I went along to Townsend's Corner and saw vehicles taking casualties to Lynn Hospital. There was a large crowd standing there, and I shall never forget the look of shock on everyone's face.

Early in the war Mr Peckover joined the Loke Road fire-watching group whose headquarters was under the sand bags I had helped to fill. He didn't last long, which wasn't surprising bearing in mind his long hours and manual work.

A lot of boys went in for making cigarette lighters. The body was a .202 cartridge case drilled and threaded at the closed end to take part of a bicycle inner-tube valve through which ran the wick. Cotton wool was stuffed inside the case, and a shorter cartridge case fitted over the bottom. Other parts like the wheel, flint and spring could be bought very cheaply and soldered on to the side of the cartridge. The wick top was kept clean and moist by a bicycle dust cap screwed over it. Most of us carried a home-made lighter with us, looking for a chance to use it.

One day we were changing, getting ready for a P.E. lesson. One boy, with his back to me, had put a lot of grease on his hair and combed it backwards so it had a sort of point of hair at the back. From this, one longer hair stuck out beyond the rest. I took my lighter, flicked it on and put the flame to the end of the single hair. Immediately a sheet of flame shot up from the whole of the boy's head. I grabbed my shirt from a bench and put it right over the boy's head, extinguishing the flame as quickly as it had begun. The boy himself hardly knew what had happened, but the others had seen it, and were all helpless with laughter. Although the flame had lasted for only a split second, the smell of burning hair was overpowering, filling the room and corridor. A minute or two later, trying to do handsprings, we could only run as far as the box before having to stop, laughing uncontrollably. One boy did get as far as the box, but his arms collapsed and he sprawled on to the mat, unable to get up for giggling. Surprisingly, and fortunately for me, no burnt hair was showing on the boy's head. I never repeated that experiment.

With aeroplanes crashing or being shot down there was a lot of perspex from windscreens about. We made holes in this, by drilling or burning with a red-hot poker, sawed round them, filed and sand-papered, and produced rings of all sizes. Spent and deformed bullets were also collected and exchanged, and we could get thousands of them from a rifle range near the River Ouse just the other side of the Cut Bridge.

Arriving home one day I was informed by Mrs Peckover that her husband had something for me that would make others turn green with envy. It was a piece of shot-down German aircraft, and shaped just like a pistol. I had a lot of offers for that.

On one other occasion when bombs had fallen on Lynn I told my hosts I was going out to look for pieces of shrapnel. After a couple of hours searching I had found only a piece of cast iron that was probably from a drain-pipe, so decided to go back and claim this as a piece of bomb. As I was waiting to cross the road at the end of South Clough Lane, opposite St James' Park, the wheel of a passing lorry threw up what looked like a large stone. It turned out to be a piece of shrapnel, so I threw away the remnant of drain-pipe and rushed back to display my find.

The notice 'Walls Have Ears' was posted all over Lynn, on the insides as well as outsides of buildings, and there was always talk of spies. Every cinema show warned that 'Careless Talk Costs Lives'. One day a well-dressed man with a new car was knocking on doors in North End trying to sell razor-blades. A group of women (all fishermen's wives, so the story went) grabbed him and held him down until the police arrived. We never heard that the man was in fact a spy, so he probably wasn't.

As well as warning about careless talk, cinemas showed lots of propaganda shorts. In one of them, at the Pilot, factory workers were complaining that what they were doing didn't help the war effort. One group was producing luxurious gloves with a mitten part which, when pulled back, exposed the tips of fingers. 'Fit for a queen, and no use for the war' was their verdict. Another group was putting together wooden boxes, of no apparent use. It turned out that the gloves were for ATS girls who operated searchlights and needed warm hands together with the possibility of operating delicate controls with their finger-tips. The boxes were to hold essential rations for service personnel. On the whole, these propaganda films were unconvincing. Once, at the Theatre Royal, some rather simple process about the manufacture of munitions was explained in some detail. At the end of this boring account a man near the front said loudly, in a very local accent:

'Ah! Now we know somethin'!' He got the best laugh of the evening.

People were aware that there was a lot of propaganda on the radio, too, because they listened to 'Lord Haw Haw' (William Joyce, who was executed after the war as a traitor). Mr and Mrs Peckover would often hear him claim that, for example, an Allied battleship had been sunk, when we had heard nothing about it on the British news. When it was followed, some time later, by an official admission, one of my hosts would say:

'There you are! Lord Haw Haw was right again!'

I called at 81, Saddlebow Road one day to see Mr Peckover's parents and, hearing they wanted the garden dug over, got a spade and spent most of the rest of the day digging. A year or so later, Mr Peckover senior was pottering about in the garden when he disturbed some bombs that had lain hidden there for a long time. At least one of them exploded, but old Mr Peckover was only slightly hurt. From the local newspaper's account of the story the bombs had fallen there before I did my digging. Although they were only small bombs, I was relieved I hadn't gone in for trenches there.

For most of the war, Lynn Town Football Club managed somehow to arrange a match nearly every Saturday. The fixtures were well advertised by posters, and as often as not the opponents were teams from the services. We saw a lot of international players at The Walks, playing for services' teams. Lynn had some notable victories, and I watched most of them. Another regular spectator was Mr Savage, who always turned up on his well-used bike.

Lynn usually had a very dependable goalkeeper, by the name of Spaxman, who hardly ever missed a game. The right winger had an unusual ploy: when tackled, he often crouched low over the ball, and his tackler went sprawling over his shoulders. He was up immediately and running goalwards. A great favourite was a stocky, bald-headed centre-half named Fakenbridge. He was a pillar of Lynn's defence, and had a habit of standing motionless, hands on knees, letting opponents' passes or shots hit his head and bounce off, turning defence into immediate attack. He must have had an uncanny sense of positioning. One day I was walking from Kettlewell Lane towards the railway footbridge when I saw someone fishing by the big pipe in the Leccy Pit. The water there was always very hot, and vapour at first obscured the angler's face, but then I saw it was Fakenbridge! He said he hadn't caught anything but, as I watched, he caught a four-ounce carp. To my disappointment he put the fish into a bag, packed his gear and cycled away. He wasn't a hero of mine after that.

During one match against a services team the referee had become very unpopular because he gave so many decisions against the Lynn team. For some reason I was on that occasion hoping the visitors would win but even I had to agree that a lot of the decisions against the Lynn team should have gone the other way. Everyone was discussing the matter during half-time, and thinking that surely things would change. But things were even worse in the second half, and the crowd was becoming quite angry. Then, in the space of a minute, the referee disallowed what was clearly a penalty to Lynn, and gave the other side a penalty for something that happened outside the penalty area and for which Lynn should have had a free kick. This was too much for one spectator who shouted to the referee:

'You rotten ol' sod, you!'

The anger was transformed into peals of laughter that lasted to the end of the match. Lynn lost, but their supporters were still giggling and smiling as they left.

During evacuation, the reason we were there was never far from anyone's thoughts, and even if nothing much happened for a whole week in Lynn, we were reminded there was a war on by the Saturday morning air raid siren practice at the electricity works.

In the Water

As far as we knew, the only person to swim in the Long Pond was the man who went in to recover his artificial worm; but a lot of local swimming did go on. People had swum in the River Ouse for generations, but that was already becoming dangerous. When swimming near the Point, north of Lynn, we would often be carried along at an alarming rate, and this fast flow was probably due to the river having been narrowed. Whilst being carried along fast I once got a nasty cut on the foot from posts - probably part of the material laid down to protect the banks from erosion. During the war there were two places in the Gaywood River for swimming; one was near the Stone Bridge on Wootton Road, and the other was at the Saunders. This latter was excellent because of its depth - five feet just below the sluice gate, where you could often see big carp swimming near the bottom. Beside this was a brick bank and, on this, some concrete posts where you could climb, balance for a moment, and jump from a height of about eight feet. When a group of a dozen or so boys descended on the Saunders to swim, it was commotion everywhere: boys jumped from the posts, from the plank bridge at the sluice and from the sides of the flotsam bin; and they dived in from any low point they could find - the favourite being the one on the opposite side by the corner of Eastgate Street. The wide part of the Saunders would be full of swimmers thrashing about and disturbing the bottom. There wasn't much fishing possible then but, an hour or two later when the water had settled down, fish returned to feed in the disturbed water and it was a promising time.

Another popular place for swimming was on the River Nar, or Setch, near South Lynn station, where the railway crossed over. When we heard a train coming we would lie on our backs and wave as the train went over. Passengers would often wave until out of sight. That was also an excellent place for roach and pike.

There was a brief revival of local swimming after the war when lower reaches of the Gaywood River were twice dredged. One new place I swam in then was next to the stile where Henry and I had caught our first gudgeon. The Saunders and Kettlewell Lane stretches were also dredged at this time, but they soon silted up again. Abstraction and pollution meant the end of swimming.

The vast majority of our contact with water was, however, of the accidental kind known as 'gettin' a wettin' '. Most common was having water over the top of your 'water boots' or Wellingtons. You had only to slip on a wet bank, or misjudge a jump over a stream to get a bootful of water. For a year or so, after the start of the war, there was a rectangular wooden construction at the edge of the Saunders. It was almost exactly level with the hole in the old town wall, and had planks round the inside rather like shelves. We used to jump from one side to the other. You had only to slip, or miss, to get your boots full of water. I often dreaded going home because of wet water boots. Mrs Peckover worried about the danger of water, and complained about having to dry off water boots every day.

When David Rose was about eight, the two of us were fishing in the Square from the railway lines. We were watching our floats and talking. David had his left hand resting on the top strand of barbed wire, when the latter suddenly snapped, and he went headlong into the water four feet below. He made a huge splash. At that time the generating station pushed water round day and night, and the current was very strong in the Square. Water came round the baffle walls and piled up at the tunnel before rushing under the railway. The water came up to the top of the tunnel at the Square, so there was little chance of survival for anyone getting into the tunnel itself, because they would have had to swim twenty yards under water before coming out into the Long Pond. David couldn't swim at all then. Fortunately I was

102

standing between David and the tunnel, and saw him screw up his face and shut his eyes as he plunged downwards. I managed to push my shoulders under the bottom wire, certain that I was too late. But I managed to grab him by his jacket. Then came a frightening few seconds when I was just managing to hold on, with David at a forty-five-degree angle, his legs pulled by the current almost into the tunnel's mouth. As far as I remember, I managed to pull him a bit higher, grab his hands, and heave him up on to the railway track. I took him back to his house, convinced his mother would be furious with me. I had, after all, taken him off fishing, and probably also decided we would fish at the Square. She knew he could never have survived the tunnel. But to my surprise, and relief, Mrs Rose was so relieved her son hadn't been drowned that she thanked me for having grabbed him in time. It was over a week later that, fishing from the Boards, I noticed something lying in the shallow water at the Loke end. I fished it out with a landing net, thus rescuing David's St James' School cap. It had returned via the tunnel and pond, to within a few feet of David's house.

(I have recently discovered that my memory was at fault in part of this story. I thought I must have pulled David out of the Square myself. But Neville Tunmore has reminded me that, unable to get David out alone, I held on to him and shouted for help. Neville, fishing just the other side of the railway, ran over and grabbed David's other hand. Together we pulled him out.)

There were two ways of getting to the Back of Leccy. One was along Littleport Street to Austin Street, over a gate, and across a couple of fields. But this wasted valuable time, especially if you had already been fishing in the Long Pond area. So the normal route was over the wall into the Side of Leccy, then around the end of a fence. This fence was made of corrugated iron, and went from the electric light building down to the bank at right angles, overhanging the water. To get round this projection you had to hold on to the corrugated iron, lean backwards over the water, and work your way round as best you could. You had to grip the end of the corrugated iron with one hand, hold your tackle in the other hand, and move your feet round between branches. There was always a moment when everything depended on keeping a grip on the end of the corrugated iron with your thumb and forefinger, with your weight pulling you outwards towards the water below. It was a difficult enough operation with both hands free but, with only one hand, it was even more tricky.

One day, Neville had been fishing at the Side of Leccy, and decided to try at the back. He collected his gear in one hand, and began going through the usual routine to get round the end of the corrugated iron. On this occasion he got both feet caught in the branches, lost his grip, and fell backwards into the water four feet below. His head and shoulders hit the water, but both feet were still trapped in the branches, and he hung there. He could see only a green, murky world, and was swallowing water at an alarming rate. After ten or fifteen seconds' struggling he managed to free his feet, and get the right way up. For some time he stood in four and a half feet of water, gasping and retching, unable to see, and still almost unable to breathe. It took him some time to recover. When he could open his eyes he saw his rod sticking out of the water some yards away, managed to grab it, and scrambled out of the water up the steep-sided bank. He didn't bother to rescue any other pieces of equipment - it had, after all, been quite an experience for a ten-year-old non-swimmer. He sloshed through the high grass and climbed over the wall, landing with a splash! on the tarmac path between Kettlewell Lane and the railway footbridge.

'Hello, Neville! Have you been fishing?'

It was Mrs Brown, a friend of his parents.

Neville, water streaming from his trousers, shoes and hair, replied that he had.

'And how is your mother? Well, I hope.'

'Yes, she's very well, thank you.'

There followed a battery of questions from Mrs Brown about Neville's parents, his sister, his brother and other members of the family to which Neville answered politely. There was soon a stream of water flowing across the path, forming a large puddle, but it wasn't until after twenty minutes of questioning that Mrs Brown said she was very busy and didn't have time to talk any more, conveyed her best wishes to Mrs Tunmore, and said goodbye to Neville.

During the conversation Mrs Brown hadn't mentioned the wet hair, wet clothes and the stream of water, and Neville didn't refer to them either. He never knew if she hadn't noticed, was too polite to talk about them, or assumed it was something to do with fishing.

Arriving home, Neville went through a familiar routine. He opened the back door and shouted:

'Mum! I fell in and got a wetting!'

'Stay outside!' ordered Mrs Tunmore in the sternest tones she could muster. 'Take those wet clothes off! And don't you dare come inside!'

Neville removed his wet clothes, received a towel, and dried himself off. Only then was he allowed in.

Nearly sixty years later Neville remembers that day well, but he's not sure if he ever conveyed Mrs Brown's message to his mother.

Trespassers

If David Rose had been alone when he fell into the Square he would almost certainly have drowned. Much younger boys fished and played there,

The tunnel at the Saunders feeding the electric light works

balancing along the narrow sides with deep water just below, and often getting on to the baffle walls. These were only a foot wide, often slippery, yet boys walked along them and, coming to the end, with water swirling round below, would lean over, and put their weight on the wall opposite. Sometimes they were stuck there, unable to push themselves back, and had to be rescued by being pulled from behind or pushed from in front. We had no right to be there really. To get in, you had to negotiate barbed wire. This got pushed down very soon after it was renewed, but it was obvious that the place was not a public one. Even to get as far as that barbed wire you had to be on the railway - which was trespassing, as at least two notices pointed out between the wire and the kissing gates. The only other way of getting inside the Square was to climb a fence along the generating station branch railway which, again, we had no right to do.

Where Neville Tunmore fell in, at the Side of Leccy, was the property of the electricity company, so was the Back of Leccy, and so was the Leccy Pit. The Square itself also belonged to them. Yet I don't think we were turned off once in all the years we fished in these places. In fact, later on a few of us were even invited to go through the generating station building so we could get to the Back of Leccy without having to negotiate the awkward fence.

We were also trespassing at the Saunders sluice gate, little bridge and the flotsam bin. At the upstream end of the flotsam bin was another tunnel into which water poured strongly, usually coming up above the top of the tunnel itself. If you got into this, there was no way of getting out unless you could survive fifty yards underwater.

105

The path in Kettlewell Lane Gardens followed the old town wall, and near where it met the path from the Long Pond was a hole. You could look down over a low wall, and see water swirling around ten feet below. This was where water arrived from the tunnel coming from just above the sluice gate. On the other side of the hole was another tunnel through which water went off under the Kettlewell Lane Path to the Side of Leccy. Between these two tunnels was a third where water went off towards the electric light works. The hole was like a small room, with vertical, stone and brick sides so, if you had fallen in there you would have stood little chance of getting out. We used occasionally to fish there, but I never knew anyone to catch anything. A year or so after the beginning of war this hole was covered over completely by heavy railings all chained into position. Overnight it became one of the safest places, because we could climb all over it without fear of falling in.

As we stood fishing at the Square, on the railway, we would have locomotives and long lines of trucks passing behind us only three feet away. Sometimes we put a coin on the rail just before the train arrived and, if it jumped off, we would reach and pull it back while the trucks were still passing. Even when the men were shunting they never worried about our being there. In fact the railway workers usually gave us a cheery wave or shout, asking what we'd caught. A lot of them were relatives or neighbours of young anglers.

The only place we had to vacate when a train came along was at the Lines. Here, along the downstream side of the bridge, was a pipe about two feet wide, with girders just in front and behind. The pipe conveyed warm water from the electric light works, and was a comfortable place to fish from. When rolling stock went along that side of the bridge it went above the pipe, so we had to move. If we didn't, the driver stopped and whistled, shouted or got down and chased us off.

One day I was fishing at the Lines beside Mr Petts' orchard when an engine came from the station direction pulling a line of trucks. When the trucks had almost passed, there were some unfamiliar noises. I looked up to see waggons careering about in different directions all over the track. In the space of seconds, wheels had been ripped off trucks; huge chains and towing hooks had been snapped; trucks had rolled across sleepers, smashing them or making deep grooves across them. Sleepers were sticking up vertically; trucks were lying on their sides; and one truck was completely turned over with its wheels in the air. If anyone had been on that side of the track they would probably have been killed.

When the incident was reported in the local paper it was claimed that the sleepers were rotten.

I was only ever challenged once and that was at the Lines Bridge. A man came from the direction of the kissing-gates carrying gardening tools. He stopped, and told me I shouldn't be there. I said I had been fishing there for years, and so had lots of other people, and nobody had said anything before. To this he replied that he couldn't do anything then, because he was not on duty. I supposed he was a policeman, perhaps a railway policeman. I never saw him again and I never heard of any other angler being challenged in the area.

The only places that we had a legal right to fish in were the Lily Pond, the Long Pond, and parts of the Gaywood River, and they were also the safest places.

Between the Swan Laundry Bridge and the bridge at River Lane in Gaywood was a metal railway bridge which we called the Black Bridge. One day a few of us were fishing there. Jammy was the only other Londoner apart from myself; all the others were Lynn boys. One of the latter dared Jammy to climb below the bridge rails and stay there while a train went over. Jammy accepted the challenge and when we saw the nearby Gaywood Road gates closing against road traffic he ran to the bridge and climbed down. It wasn't a very fast train, but it thundered over the little bridge. Jammy didn't come up immediately, and we ran on to the line to see if he was all right. He looked up at us with a white face, and began climbing out. He walked along the few feet of line with wobbly legs and sat down on the grass. The experience had really shaken him. Some time later I thought of doing the same thing myself. When I knew a train was coming along I went on to the bridge and began climbing down. It was only then that I realised how confined the space was. Even crouching as low as you could, you were only inches below the rails. I decided against it, and withdrew. There was, later, the story of a boy who tried to emulate Jammy, but had been so frightened as the train went over that he scrambled out below the rails and dropped into the river. I didn't blame him.

Dogs

'Bob's in!'

When we were fishing in the Long Pond we knew what that meant: Bob, a black Labrador, had got into the water and was on his way, swimming strongly down the pond. There was no point in leaving your tackle out because not only was Bob likely to snap at a float, but he would also disturb the water so much that the fish took half an hour to get over the commotion. When Bob went in, we hauled out.

Bob could arrive at any time, on any day of the week. He always got in at the railway end, where the fences went out from the sides, and swam towards the Loke. He occasionally veered to the right or left, and climbed out, with young anglers fleeing before him in all directions so as to get out of range of the surprising amount of water he could get rid of in half a dozen rapid shakes. But usually Bob swam the whole length of the pond, getting out at the

Loke end - which would already have been vacated by anyone fishing there. Bob wasn't the only dog to swim in the Long Pond; several others had an occasional dip, but they tended to swim out and back, not disturb the whole place.

Bob was only one of scores of dogs that paid visits to the Long Pond. Many were put out in the morning and not expected home until evening, between which times they roamed over large tracts of town and countryside. It wasn't often I went anywhere without recognising one or two dogs, giving them a stroke and a pat, and seeing them go busily on their way. It was a big contrast to London, where dogs had been few and far between.

Many dogs that passed the pond were regular - almost as regular as the people who walked or cycled past on their way to or from work or shopping. The regular dogs knew they might be offered bread, paste, a chip or some other bait, getting a stroke at the same time. Our bait must often have smelt of dog, but the Long Pond fish were used to that.

Conventional angling wisdom has it that you never take a dog with you when fishing because of the disturbance. This didn't apply at the Long Pond. Many households were minus men of military age so, when dogs were taken out it was often children who took them. It was normal for young anglers to arrive at the pond with the family dog.

Several local residents had dogs. The Rose family had Gyp, a friendly dog that knew everyone and wouldn't roam far. Mr Tunmore used to take his black Labrador, Roger, with him when he went eel-holing. Returning home one day he left his bait, an old piece of fish, on the hook, and leant his rod against a wall. Later, hearing whining and thrashing noises, he rushed outside to see Roger dragging the rod along the garden path. He had sniffed at the fish and hooked himself. Mr Tunmore quickly found some wire-cutters, managed to grab the dog's collar, cut the treble at the top, and slid the hook out of the poor animal's nostrils.

Mick belonged to a family in Smith Avenue and had been around for years. I found him by the pond late one evening and tried to take him off with me to Smith Avenue on my way home. He refused, and eventually disappeared into the Tunmores' garden. The next day I found out that Mick had changed hands, and now belonged to Chris Tunmore. Such changes of ownership were quite common. Chris was so attached to Mick that, when the dog died, he had another called Mick. Chris Tunmore was also on friendly terms with a dog called Titch who lived in a house in Woodwark Avenue. If anyone else spoke to Titch, or tried to stroke him, or even offer him food, he would snarl or bite. But he accepted Chris, and would sit with him for hours on the banks of the Lily Pond.

One of the dogs that used to wander past the Long Pond was a whippet called Prince. He belonged to Mr Knights - host of the evacuee who called him 'Knights'. Prince was never a very sociable dog, but would stand there to be stroked for a limited time and could, occasionally, be persuaded to eat a piece of bait. Several years after the war I was walking by the River Setch, and met a whippet that looked like a very old Prince. When I spoke to him and called 'Prince', he looked up, brightened and wagged his tail. Although not walking very well he followed me all the way back to Smith Avenue. When I knocked at the door, Mr Knights himself opened it, and I asked if the dog was indeed Prince. He nodded, and the dog went indoors. Mr Knights said:

'And who might you be, then?' He had completely forgotten me, but his dog hadn't.

One remarkable Long Pond dog was Chum. He belonged to Alan (Pluck) Hemeter who lived on the banks of the Lily Pond in Townshend Terrace. If you threw a brick or lump of concrete into the pond, Chum would go in, get it in his mouth, and bring it ashore. He must have known things weigh less in water! Chum didn't like burning cigarette ends, and would pounce on them, knocking them about with paws and nose until he put them out.

My friendship with another 'Prince', a Welsh collie, lasted for many years, and I knew him from when he was a puppy. I got him to swim by pushing him into shallow ditches, and once he could swim it was impossible to keep him out of water. He loved walks along the Gaywood River, Salter's Road, Wootton and the marshes where we would sometimes spend all day.

At one time a dog called Whiskey lived nearby, and he sometimes used to accompany me and Prince. To avoid being knocked over when I fed them on our walks, I used to stand on a stile or post, out of their reach, and throw food down to them. They were more excited than usual whenever we came to a stile or thick fence post but, once they had been fed, they knew stiles and posts didn't mean food any more.

Prince (left) and Whiskey (right)

We were returning one day from the marshes, and had just passed Southgate's shop when Whiskey saw a dog on Peck's Field. Without looking, he bolted across the road towards it. An elderly man on a bicycle, handlebars laden with shopping bags, was coming from the town direction and, as Whiskey ran across, the man's front wheel hit him dead centre. Man, bike and shopping hit the ground. Whiskey forgot the other dog on Peck's Field, and ran. In seconds he was out of sight round the Raby Avenue bend. The man, lying on his back, raised his head and looked about him to see burst bags of flour and custard powder, spilled vegetables, and apples in the gutter. He let out a loud groan, and laid his head back on to the road. I rushed over and helped him up, got him to the pavement and rescued his bike. Several of us collected what shopping was saveable. When the man had recovered he asked me if I had seen the dog or knew where it came from. I thought it wisae to use my Lynn accent.

'I haven't never seen it afore, but he run off that way.'

I pointed towards the Lily Pond instead of Raby Avenue. The man eyed the remnants of his shopping.

'I'd like to find the ruddy owner, that I would.'

I nodded towards Prince who was sitting on the pavement, watching.

'I'm glad my dog don't run across roads like that.'

Whiskey didn't venture out again until the next day. Like so many of the dogs I knew he was a loveable coward.

Some years after the war, when I used to spend time in Lynn and London alternately, it was heartbreaking for me, and I think for Prince, when I left for London. But when I arrived in Lynn for a stay there were happy reunions. Once, while I was away, his owners moved to Gaywood. I found their address and went there. They now lived in a long road and, as I turned into it, there were lots of children, adults and dogs moving about. But then came frantic barking from a hundred yards along the road. It was Prince, who nearly knocked me over in his delight.

Rivals to the Long Pond

I often helped Mr Peckover to feed his poultry and rabbits. One day, he asked me to go into the garden with him, as he had something to show me. It was a young rabbit, almost entirely black. I was trying to make friends with it when Mr Peckover said he had bought it for me. I had my own rabbit! When we went upstairs again, Mrs Peckover said:

'Oh well, I expect fishing will take second place now!'

It was soon clear that I was expected to feed my rabbit in the evenings, and I did so for a week. Then, rushing off to the pond one evening, I forgot. It happened again, and again. My hosts were both disappointed. Soon, Mr Peckover was feeding my rabbit most of the time and, eventually, I left it to him entirely. One day he told me that my rabbit was no longer there, in its hutch. He had sold it. Mrs Peckover told me it was my own fault for not doing the feeding regularly. I was sorry the rabbit had gone but, on the other hand, glad that I could rush off in the evening with a clear conscience. Fishing could never have taken second place.

Somehow I had become a member of the Boys' Brigade. It was nothing to do with the attraction of wearing a belt and cap uniform; more to do with being persuaded at the St John's Church Sunday School. My hosts were pleased I had joined, and proudly told their friends I had joined the 'Church Lads' Brigade'.

On my way to the first meeting, feeling conspicuous in uniform, I avoided the Long Pond area by going along Gaywood Road, and turned right into Austin Street by Chilver's bike shop. My destination was a frail-looking old building a little way along on the left, with small, leaded windows and narrow, rickety stairs. Drill sessions took place in a large space upstairs. I was asked to stand in a corner to see the sort of things that went on. At a sudden, loud command that made me jump, the other boys quickly lined up in twos. To a series of other shouts they began marching around, turning left and right, arms swinging up to shoulder height, and feet thumping. The building swayed and shook. Dust came up from the floor and down from the ceiling. When the boys came to a sudden halt the whole place moved so alarmingly I was sure it was about to collapse. Even more striking were the expressions on the boys' faces. At Sunday School they had been a quiet, friendly and rather giggly lot. Now they scowled, looked fierce, angry, determined, and even cruel. They looked, to quote one of Mr Peckover's sayings, as though 'they could hang their own grandmothers'.

It was a cold, wet evening, but my mind went to the Back of Leccy only a hundred yards away the other side of Austin Street. Roach, carp and pike would all be there, safe and happy in their warm water. How I longed to be there! Fortunately, I wasn't expected to take part on this first evening, so could appreciate the amusing sight of the dust, now like a thick fog, and the white-covered boys, many of them coughing and sneezing because of the dust. At the end of the session I didn't go back via Littleport Street, but made my way in the dark through fields to the Back of Leccy. Here, everything was quiet except for an occasional lap of water and the wind sighing in the row of willow trees. I crept over the plank bridge, negotiated the corrugated iron fence at the Side of Leccy, and went home via the Long Pond.

Mr and Mrs Peckover asked me lots of questions about what happened, and I tried to describe the evening without letting them know how horrified I had been. But I couldn't sound favourable because I knew I'd never go there again. The following week, while the drill session was held again, I went along to the Back of Leccy. I could appreciate even more than usual how lucky I was to be there, and not among those stern faces doing drill just the other side of Austin Street.

It was the vicar of St John's who called one day at number 23 to collect my uniform but, being out at the time, I didn't have to explain.

My sister and I had always gone to Sunday School in London, and I continued in Lynn at St John's Church, getting two prizes for attendance. It was always a rush to get there on the Sunday afternoon, but the return was more leisurely and interesting. My first stop was the Gaywood river a short distance from the church. There was the sluice gate with, in spring, its thousands of darning needles climbing up; there was the deeper water coming from under the station; there were the more open stretches where roach abounded; and there was the water between swimming pool and bandstand where large carp could often be seen lying just below the surface. It was a short walk from there to the Swan Laundry Bridge, and on to the Long Pond.

One summer afternoon I dallied at the Long Pond longer than usual before Sunday School, and knew I'd have to run all the way. Then I saw friends fishing at the Lines, and ran down there to see what was happening. Lots of big carp were lying under the bridge, and I watched them for a while, seeing some well over eight pounds. It was now past three o'clock. I had never skipped Sunday School before, but decided to do so now.

I watched the carp the following Sunday afternoon, and the next. After that I began leaving home with a linewinder, float and hook in one pocket and, in the other, some bread bait. From then on I spent Sunday afternoons lying on the Lines railway bridge fishing by hand between the lines. The carp were too shy, but I caught small gudgeon and the occasional roach. Head down below the railway lines, with only legs visible, I knew I wouldn't be recognisable from Dodman's Bridge or even from between the kissing-gates. When I eventually told Mr and Mrs Peckover I didn't want to go to Sunday School any more, they didn't raise any objection, or even look surprised. Perhaps they had already guessed.

One day I was fishing from the Boards when the shout of 'Reg!' came from behind. Mrs Rose, in the front garden of Kano, was waving me over. She told me that people running a shop just off Norfolk Street were looking for a boy of my age to do deliveries for them, and she had suggested me. I thanked her and said I would be very interested. It would bump up my pocket-money, and make affordable all kinds of fishing equipment. Mrs Rose passed the word on, and I went and saw the people advertising the job. The hours were evenings after school and on Saturday. The people were very nice, and it was agreed I should start in ten days' time. Mr and Mrs Peckover were pleased, and I was looking forward to starting. Apart from the money I'd be able to ride the delivery bike around the Pond and be the envy of everyone.

There were three days to go before I started, and I was fishing off the Point. It had been a very successful week's fishing. I had caught a tench in the Lily Pond, five carp in the Long Pond, several carp in the Square, Side of Leccy and Back of Leccy, and decent roach at the Lines and the Saunders. What a week!

112

As I thought about the last seven days, I realised I had been spending more time fishing even than usual. Out of school hours I had done nothing but fish. It had been wonderful. Then I understood why I had been fishing so much. It was because I knew there was going to be much less time for fishing. Only Sunday left! I couldn't stand that!

When I explained to Mr and Mrs Peckover that I couldn't take the job after all, I thought they would advise me to try it for a short time to see how it worked out. But they didn't. They were sympathetic. I did hope that one of them would offer to go and explain at the shop, but neither of them did. It was the day I was to start that I managed to drag myself to the shop in the little alleyway between Townshend's Corner and Austin Street. I didn't manage the explanation very well, and the lady I spoke to wasn't very pleased. But when it was done, and I was outside, I sprinted home in high spirits. Another narrow escape.

The only thing I cannot remember about that job was how much I was to earn. It obviously wasn't the important part.

Hosts of Problems

Every day we heard of people being killed and injured as a result of the war, yet as far as I was concerned some wonderful things were happening. Many people I had met in Lynn would, I knew, be lifelong friends. I had got to know the Long Pond and the other beautiful waters, with their wonderful fish. So, early on, I had the feeling that, for me, everything was for the best in the best of all possible worlds.

Once, during a lunch break at school, Smithy and I were chatting to Mr Bone. The topic of billets cropped up and, at one point, the teacher said to Smithy:

'That's a marvellous billet you've got there, Smithy!'

Smithy agreed that it was. With my Panglossian philosophy I firmly believed I had the best of all possible billets and hosts, and waited for Mr Bone to say the same thing to me. To my surprise he didn't, and the conversation drifted on to something else. It wasn't as if Mr Bone didn't know Mr and Mrs Peckover, or 23, Mill Houses, he did. I concluded that Smithy's hosts must be special friends of his.

There were, however, two occasions later in the war when my stay with Mr and Mrs Peckover could have come to a sudden end, and when I had to question exactly what 'everything for the best' really meant. The first time was perhaps almost inevitable bearing in mind our three personalities.

Mr Peckover was a practical man. He did our boot and shoe repairs, mended and built bikes, put up sheds and extensions on to them, looked after his poultry and rabbits and did the gardening. He did perfect 'knotless' bindings. All this practical work, in the days before DIY, he did with the barest and cheapest materials. He could also draw and paint well, though he never had time to practise. Later, when work with horses all but disappeared, he got a job with a local brewery where his talents were soon recognised and he was given the job of repairing and renovating brewery properties. With practical things he could foresee problems, had endless patience and never lost his temper whatever the snags. With people he was friendly, and very generous, but he could also be impatient, dogmatic and intolerant. When he took a dislike to anyone it was permanent. He always claimed he wasn't sorry when a neighbour, with whom he had had an argument, died. He could lose his temper with people.

Mrs Peckover was also practical in that she worked hard and regularly at the housework. She got up early to do this, but was often doing it at other times of the day, although she professed to hate housework. She was an excellent cook, and always prompt with meals. With people she was more tactful and patient than her husband.

The relevant trait of my own personality, as far as this episode is concerned, is that I was very untidy, and my bedroom was usually in a mess.

One day the three of us were having a meal, and the conversation briefly touched the state of my room. The hundreds of spent cartridge cases, and rifle bullets I had collected over the years had spilled out on to the floor, and I had pushed them out of sight under the bed and washstand. I agreed to collect them up and put them into a large box, then the conversation moved onto other things. Towards the end of the meal Mrs Peckover reminded me about the cartridges, and hadn't finished talking when, to my amazement, Mr Peckover jumped out of his low armchair and hit me with considerable force on the side of the head. Since I hadn't the faintest idea what it was about I grabbed him and we wrestled across the room knocking things off the table as we did so. I soon found myself in a very advantageous position, sitting on the chaise-longue, holding his waistcoat, legs bent at the knees and feet firmly against his stomach. We were face to face, and I mouthed a swear word at him. In our scuffle we had pushed the chaise-longue hard against a wall, and I knew I could win the encounter. All I had to do was kick hard with my legs, and he would go staggering backwards against their bedroom door about six feet behind him. If I pushed hard enough the bedroom door would certainly give way, and he would go with it, probably hitting a chest of drawers just inside the bedroom. With my opponent disposed of for a few seconds I would rush to the window behind me, open it and jump twelve feet into the soft soil of a garden below. I had often done this from a back window when nobody was about, practising parachute jumps. Mr Peckover wouldn't be able to emulate my exit and, by the time he had negotiated the stairs, I would be out of sight. I could outrun him anyway.

All this was clear to me in the second or two we eyed each other. I knew from my wrestling that it would be easy. But what then? He, having been kicked half the length of the flat, would never agree to my return. That would be the end. He could never bury the hatchet after having lost what looked like being the only round. And this could be my chance to get back home, to London. But what did my theory of 'everything for the best' really mean? Did it mean that if I went back to London the mere fact of it having happened made it the best? Or did it mean, as I had understood it up to now, that what had already happened was for the best, and any change must be for the worse? And what about the Long Pond, the Gaywood River and my friends the fish? What would life be like without them?

There was an alternative. I could run off to a teacher, or even the police, explain what had happened, and ask for another billet. I could hardly hope for one as close to the Long Pond, but it would be better than not being able to fish at all. What would my philosophy mean then? Would a different billet be automatically for the best? Suppose I had hosts who were unfriendly? Or who didn't want an evacuee? Or who drank?

These thoughts took only a second or two, and I had now decided. I would win the contest, change billets and hope that would be the best of all possible worlds. I pulled Mr Peckover closer, roughly, by his waistcoat, bent my knees more, and prepared for the violent kick with both legs. But at that very moment he let go of me, and stepped back. I released his waistcoat, and he walked round the table to his low armchair. I also sat down at the table. During the whole incident Mrs Peckover, apart from uttering a shriek when her husband had swung the blow at me, had taken no part at all. She sat at the table looking horrified. She now stood, picked some things up from the floor, put them back onto the table, and sat down. We all began eating again, and finished the meal in silence.

I never found out what exactly had made Mr Peckover lose his temper because the matter was never discussed - at least when I was there. I suspect Mrs Peckover spoke about it with her husband, though.

I afterwards wondered what went on in their minds during the skirmish. Were their thoughts anything like mine?

It was several days later that I got round to clearing up the cartridge cases and bullets and, although I must have been as untidy as ever, nothing more was ever said about it.

My stay was threatened to be cut short on only one other occasion. That time it was a difference between Mrs Peckover and me, Mr Peckover having no part in it. I have no recollection of what it was about. All I can remember is being in the lavatory, and Mrs Peckover choosing that moment to bring matters to a head. Standing the other side of the lavatory door, she said:

'I'm just putting on my coat to go and see Mr Bone!' I remained silent. 'Well, do you want me to go?'

Again I said nothing. I was prepared to let whatever happened to be for the best.

'Well, do you want me to go or not? You'll have to say one way or the other!'

I said, truthfully: 'I don't know.'

Mrs Peckover eventually went away. When I came out of the lavatory she was busy in the kitchen.

Nothing more was ever said about that incident either.

Big'uns that Got Away

It was a hot, summer afternoon, and a few of us were fishing where the grass bank was widest near the Tunmores' house. None of us had had a bite, and we didn't expect anything in such conditions, so we were having cycle races, playing cricket and wrestling. The water was calm, and even the little 'uns seemed to have gone to sleep. Suddenly there was a shout:

'Your float, Reg!'

I stopped wrestling, ran blindly along the bank, slithered down to the water's edge and grabbed my rod. It was a big one; most unexpected on such a day. When we got a sight of it I could see it was the biggest I had ever hooked, perhaps about seven pounds. Eppy had my landing net but, even with the fish almost exhausted, he couldn't get it into the net. Everyone was soon trying to find a larger landing net, but they were all the same size as mine, and nowhere near big enough to take the fish. In the end, Eppy said he would try to land it using the net and his hands. He took off socks and shoes, and waded into the water. Amidst loud splashing noises Eppy did his best to get the fish on to the bank then, after a particularly fierce bout of splashing, he shouted:

'That's gone, Reg!'

But I could still feel the fish, and kept a steady pull.

'That's no good, Reg! It's gone!'

But I could still feel it. 'That haven't gone! He's still on!'

'Stop pullin', Reg, that's gone!'

'I can feel 'im, Eppy!'

'That ent the fish, Reg, that's my finger!' I stopped pulling, horrified.

'That's a bit better, Reg!'

Eppy was chuckling as he climbed up the bank, holding the line.

'Thought you was goin' to land me then, Reg!'

We all crowded round, surprised he was not dancing in agony. He soon had the hook out of his finger. It hadn't gone right in because he had managed to grab the line further up, and take most of the pull there.

We estimated the fish at seven to eight pounds. I was disappointed I hadn't landed it, and decided to get a bigger net.

Months later, on a dark, cold evening, I was fishing in the Square from the railway lines. I had had one or two bites, but caught nothing and, at times, was more interested in the shunting going on behind me than in the float. Then I had a bite, struck, and knew immediately it was a big fish. I played it for some time before getting it near the surface, and could see in spite of the dim light that it was the biggest carp I had ever seen. It looked about ten pounds, and I hadn't yet got a larger landing net. When the fish was utterly exhausted I tried netting it. But its tail was as big as my landing-net. Eventually two railwaymen came up, and exclaimed in surprise when they saw the size of the fish.

'Never seen a fish like that afore!' said one.

One of the men tried using the landing net, but it was impossible. Then the other man bent forward.

'Hold you on! I'll get it!'

He had a shunting pole and went to push the large, metal, spiral end down the fish's mouth - which was so large I was sure the spiral end would go right down into the fish's stomach.

'No!' I yelled. 'Leave it alone! You'll injure it!'

I aimed a kick at the shunting pole, and it hit the concrete side. There was a ping! and the fish was off. It righted itself and swam slowly away. The other railwayman exclaimed and put a hand to his neck.

'I'm hooked!'

When the other man shone a torch on his colleague's neck, we could see that my hook, which had been pulled from the fish's mouth, had flicked upwards into the man's flesh. But it was only the tip, and it came away easily. It was just like the previous largest fish I had hooked, couldn't land, and had lost because of not having a big enough landing net. Again someone had got the hook in him, and again he was only lightly hooked.

The two railwaymen laughed about the incident, were sympathetic, and were still talking about the great size of the fish as they walked off into the gloom. I was disappointed at losing such a large fish, but relieved it hadn't been injured by the shunting pole, and very pleased it wasn't swimming about with a hook in its mouth. Two days later I did buy a new landing net. It was circular with four sections, and was the largest one I had ever seen. When I began using it, it produced a lot of laughs. But I didn't mind that; I was looking forward to the next real big 'un.

Galloping Horses

A year or two after the beginning of the war the council stopped repairing the high, wire-netting fence by number one Harecroft Parade where the Tunmores lived, and this permanent gap encouraged people to take a short cut through there, and along Harecroft Parade to get between the kissing-gates and the

117

Loke. I was sorry about this because the grass soon became worn, and what had been a quiet few yards of bank now had people and bikes going along it. One day I was fishing from high up the bank, next to the gap, when there was a voice from behind:

'And how long have *you* been fishing?'

It was a Norfolk accent. I had never seen the man before. When I told him it had been about two years, he looked surprised.

'Really? Is that all? By the way you just cast out I'd have thought it was much longer than that!'

He moved off towards the Loke, a carrier bag in each hand. A lady whom I took to be his wife, also carrying shopping, was walking beside him.

A couple of days later he was back at the pond, this time with an expensive rod and tackle. His name was Ted High. He was twenty-nine years old at the time, but looked older. He had badly injured an arm in a fall, so was unfit for military service and most other kinds of work, and was one of the few adults who fished regularly. He preferred the company of others, and fished especially in the evenings and at week-ends, when we could all get there.

Ted was a compulsive talker, especially about fishing. He told us about the latest fishing tackle available, which was cheapest, the best baits and where the big fish were to be found. We already knew this, but it was a change having an adult interested in the same things as we were, and we soon realised he enjoyed giving advice and telling us things. Once, when he had hooked a carp in the Long Pond he handed his rod to Neville, who was not much more than seven years old.

'Here, Neville, you take over.'

Neville proceeded to play and land the fish under Ted's careful guidance.

Ted arrived about the same time as another adult, Len, who lived in Harewood Parade. Strangely, Len had also been injured in a fall, and was unfit for military service or work. Len was also keen on fishing, and had the first metal rod I had ever seen. It had long, stand-off rings - another first in the area. Ted and Len became firm friends, and were often fishing together. But their personalities were very different. Whereas Ted always talked, Len preferred to listen and remain silent. Ted was sociable but Len liked being alone. And Len was a very mild person whereas Ted would often act the hard man in spite of his bad arm.

One day some of us were fishing from near the Tunmores' house when Ted brought up the topic of a man's strength as compared with that of a woman. He stated that there was no real comparison, and that very weak men were almost always stronger than very strong women. Len wasn't so sure, and thought that women were stronger than was generally recognised. He quoted a case he had heard about on the radio where a woman had been attacked by a man, but had fought back and managed to escape. Ted was angry.

118

'That's a load of nonsense! Men are built differently. They've got bigger shoulders, stronger arms and legs. Why do you think men and women are separated for football, rugby and athletics?'

Len smiled.

'That's only convention. Men don't want to be shown up. They're the ones who organise all these sports, remember.'

Ted began to swear. 'Look! A bloody man can get hold of a bloody woman and do what he bloody likes! He can knock her out, hang her on a bloody coat-hook - hang her out the bloody window if he wants!'

But Len was adamant. 'You just try it, Ted. You'd find you can't do it. Even if it's a small woman she'd struggle and kick, and you wouldn't be able to get her near a window, let alone hang her out of it.'

'Right,' said Ted. 'How much do you want to bet?'

Len shook his head. 'It's not the sort of thing you can demonstrate, is it?'

'You put your money down and I'll demonstrate,' insisted Ted.

'Well, which woman are you going to hang out of which window?'

'I'll hang my own wife out of my own window! Just put your money down!'

Ted and his wife lived in a top flat in Harecroft Gardens, just at the back of the Tunmores' house. If we moved along the bank a few yards we could see Ted's window. But Len was shaking his head.

'Do you think I'm going to pay you for trying to hang your own wife out the window? She'd probably throw you out instead. And you know as well as I do what can happen to people who fall out of windows.'

Ted went right up to Len, and we thought there was going to be a fight.

'Right! You don't have to pay me! I'll bloody show you for nothing!'

Leaving his rod and tackle he strode off towards the Loke. We knew it would take him only a few minutes to get home. After a minute or so Len said: 'Here! Look after the rods! I'm going to stop him!'

He ran off towards the Loke.

We left the rods and kept an eye on Ted's windows from near the Tunmores' house, but nothing seemed to be happening. It was about an hour later that both men reappeared, smiling. We asked them what had happened, but they would at first say nothing. Then Len said he had taken back what he said about the strength of women, and that usually men were stronger. We were all rather disappointed.

When Neville's older brother got married he and his wife lived for a time in the flat below the one occupied by Ted and his wife. Once, over something quite trivial, Ted shouted to Neville's brother:

'If you're not careful I'll come down there and sort you out!'

I often wonder what might have happened if Ted's challenge had been taken up.

One day several of us were fishing at the Lines. Ted was doing most of the talking and, as usual, using some choice swear words. He had just strung several fluently together when a voice came from the other side of the hedge.

'Will you shut your filthy mouth! The air reeks blue round here whenever you're about! We can't come into the garden without hearing your voice and your language! There are children here, too! If I have any more I'll come round and shut your mouth for you. I can do it, don't worry!'

There was complete silence for at least fifteen minutes. Then Ted said, in a whisper: 'Who was that?'

I was the only one who knew.

'It's Mr Bone, one of our teachers. He lives there in Homelands Road.'

Ted was still whispering. 'What does he teach?'

Mr Bone was really a teacher of French and English but, since Mr Williams, the P.T. teacher, had gone back to London, Mr Bone had been pressed into taking our form for P.T. and games. I said:

'He takes Physical Training.'

Ted visibly paled. Later, as we walked away along the lines, after an hour's silence, Ted said: 'Well, he decided against coming round, didn't he?'

Ted had come out of it as best he could, but I never again heard him swear at the Lines.

Ted and Len were one day fishing at the Lines together when Len hooked something big, and eventually landed a fifteen-pound carp. Instead of putting it back, he took it to the Duke's Head Hotel and sold it. We were all sad. That fish must have been around for years. It was certainly older than we were, and perhaps older than Len himself. Ted, too, disapproved, and would have put the fish back if he had caught it. As he said:

'Well, I can't say a lot about it because Len's my friend.'

Ted was usually good-natured and would do anything for anyone. But he did get annoyed from time to time, even about fishing. One evening, the two of us were fishing a few yards apart on the Harewood Parade side. It was dark, and Len had come out of his house to chat. From where we were it wasn't possible to use the reflection of a lighted window or lamp-post to show up bites, so I was using the technique of looking slightly to the side of the float. I caught a carp of four and a half pounds, and put it in the keep-net. Not long after that I struck again and landed a three-pounder. Ted shouted:

'You're doing well tonight.'

About half an hour later I caught another carp, this time nearly five pounds. Ted said:

'How are you doing it? We've both got the same bait, haven't we?'

We were both fishing with boiled potato. I told Ted about looking to the side of the float, but he had never thought much of the idea. Perhaps he didn't have as good night vision as I had. It was less than half an hour later that I caught another carp, this time about four pounds in weight. Ted shouted:

'What's wrong with me? Why aren't I catching them? We've got the same bait, and he's only a few yards away!'

Len said something about strange things happening when fishing. I returned the fish to the far end of the pond because there was no room left in the keep-net, and resumed fishing. Only a few minutes later I hooked another fish, and was playing it. This was too much for Ted.

'Damn this! I'm not stopping here while he's catching fish all the time, and I'm not even getting a bite!'

With that, he reeled in and went home. The next day he was his normal self again.

'Well, you certainly had a good night, Reg!' And he was genuinely sorry when I told him I'd caught no more after he had left the previous evening.

One day I arrived at the Long Pond and saw Ted fishing near the Point. I went over to tackle up where he was sitting, and asked him if he'd caught anything. He replied with a string of oaths. When I asked him what the matter was he replied:

'When people like you learn a little bit they think they know it all!'

The day before we had been on perfectly good terms, so I was at a loss to understand what had happened. Ted wouldn't say anything further, so I went and fished elsewhere. For several months we avoided fishing together. When I was with others, and they talked to Ted, I remained in the background, and he ignored me too. I assumed it was to be a permanent arrangement. But one day I was going along the Lines to fish at the bridge when I saw Ted coming towards me. As we drew level he stopped and, to my surprise, spoke.

'I've been defending you, Reg, from all the things they've been saying about you.' Seeing my puzzled look, he went on: 'They've been saying you're the one who's been catching all the fish and not putting them back. But I told them you always put your fish back.'

I thanked him, although I couldn't imagine who might think I didn't put fish back. The last I hadn't returned were the three one-and-a-half-pounders from the Square, but that was a long time before Ted had appeared on the scene. I never did find out what had annoyed Ted in the first place, but at least we were on talking terms again.

At one stage Ted began to go fishing alone, often late at night or early in the morning when nobody else was about. At first he wasn't very successful; he caught a few fish, but no more than he had been catching before. Then one day he arrived at the pond very excited about a fish that had broken him up the previous night.

'This weren't one of your ten-pounders! Yet fifteen! That 15-pounder of Len's took him bootiful! Smooth as anything. This was different - wham! and he was gone! Broke me just like that!'

We were all very interested.

A week or two later Ted was telling us about another big fish that had broken him up.

'They're not fifteen-pounders! Yet twenty! They're completely different! There's no stopping them! They're like galloping horses!'

Soon, during his night and early morning fishing Ted had had encounters with these huge fish nearly everywhere. They never went off smoothly, as fish normally did, but with a series of rapid jerks that broke any tackle. Ted still came fishing during the day, but with heavy tackle and huge baits, saying that if any of the monsters were around during the day he didn't want to lose them. He had almost lost interest in the size of the carp we caught - in fact he didn't seem to be interested in anything under twenty pounds. Since Ted's descriptions of these fish that got away were always similar, he soon became known as 'Galloping Horses'.

We were all very excited about it. Ted was an experienced angler, and had caught a lot of carp. He spent more time fishing than most people, and had hooked his galloping horses in the middle of the night, or early in the morning, when we were asleep. How exciting that such mysterious and enormous monsters might exist. And we liked the idea of them being able to avoid capture. I for one began to hope these great fish would never be caught, or even seen. Let the water keep its secrets! Every two or three weeks over a period of a year, Ted told us about the latest galloping horse and, eventually, he seemed almost resigned to their being uncatchable.

The Saunders, showing sluice gate and plank bridge with the end of the flotsam bin, all now gone.

At that time one good place to see big carp moving about was at the Saunders. But you had to be there very early in the morning. In summer, and perhaps in winter also, for all we knew, they did a migration from the station area, along by the old town wall, under Highgate Bridge as far as the Saunders. For a time the Saunders itself, and halfway along towards Highgate Bridge, would be alive with large carp. They would jump out, and swirl near the surface. The reeds along by the Eastgate Street back gardens would swish and move about as fish plunged through them. Any bread that had been thrown into the water by local residents would be swallowed up, to the accompaniment of loud sucking noises.

I only made it early enough to the Saunders a few times. Once, it was at four o'clock in the morning. I didn't catch anything, but it was a fascinating two hours. Once, I arrived at six a.m. It was already light, and Ted was there, halfway between the sluice and Kettlewell Lane. I crept carefully up.

'Caught anything, Ted?'

'Not yet, Reg, but they're still about.'

'How long have you been here?'

'Got here at half past three.'

Ted was fishing with floating bread, out in the widest part of the Saunders. We both knew that the chances of catching anything were diminishing fast, and the fish would soon be on their way back towards the station. I hadn't been watching for more than a minute when a carp came slowly up to the bread, sucked it down and made off. To my amazement Ted gasped and held the fish, letting no line out at all. The rod tip plunged down, and something had to give. It was Ted's line that went, somewhere near the reel.

'He's broken me!' exclaimed Ted.

A two-pounder would have broken him if he'd tried to stop him like that.

Then I saw a coil of Ted's nylon line on the surface, not far out. One end of it was streaking away as the carp made for Highgate Bridge. I shouted:

'Your line, Ted! There! Get it!'

Ted thrust the end of his rod into the water and waved it about.

'Where? Where?'

But Ted hadn't seen his line and, within seconds, the end of it had whipped off downstream. Even if Ted had managed to get his line around the end of the rod he would no doubt have been broken up again, with no line to let out.

I couldn't understand why Ted had panicked like that. He had caught lots of carp. Why hadn't he let it have its run, and played it in the normal way? You couldn't just drag in a fish of five to six pounds.

A day or two later I heard that Ted had been telling the story of how he had been broken up again by a galloping horse in the Saunders on floating bread. Fortunately, Ted hadn't told anyone I had been present, so I kept

123

quiet. It had been a nice fish, but I had seen it clearly and would put it at no more than seven pounds. Perhaps Ted hadn't seen the fish at all, only felt it. It was very disappointing. Did those mysterious monsters not exist at all? Had Ted been trying to pull out fish without playing them? A three-pounder could feel like a galloping horse if it wasn't given its run. I still wanted to think Ted had done battle with some real monsters, but nobody else ever encountered any. Not long after that Saunders incident Ted moved away. We never found out where he went. He must have missed the fish and fishing, as it meant as much to him as it did to us. How could he bear to leave such a place?

The only thing we ever heard was that he and his wife had been divorced - an unusual thing in those days. Perhaps he had tried hanging her out of the window!

Rendez-vous for Chat

The bracket that held my broken bike frame together began to loosen, and Mr Peckover reckoned it wouldn't last much longer. He said it was time for another frame, and he brought one home only a day or two later. It was enormous, and felt like twice the weight of the other one. The bottom bracket was yellowish, as if it was made from brass. Mr Peckover thought it might have been a policeman's bike frame. My host was often talking about a breed of rabbits called 'Norfolk Giant', and that's what I decided to call my new bike.

The Norfolk Giant was comfortable as well as strong, and I never envied others their sports models. It didn't have a three-speed, but I didn't feel the need for that. The only person I envied was Jammy. He had handlebars that I had only ever seen once before. They had stem brakes, but were very slightly dropped - rather like my own old handlebars turned upside down. Several times I offered to buy those handlebars, or do a part exchange, but Jammy was never willing. When he went back to London, taking his bike with him, I assumed that was the end of the matter. (I was wrong. Just after the war I happened to meet Jammy in London, repeated my offer, and got them.)

Nearly everyone used a bike, even some very elderly people who hardly went fast enough to remain upright. Mr and Mrs Peckover seldom went on a bus or train, and used bikes for most of their travels in Lynn and to villages even up to ten miles away. There was not much traffic on the roads, and practically no private cars.

Around the Long Pond every kind of bike wheel could be seen from the tiny ones of children's bikes to the twenty-eight by one and a half so common at the time. Bikes were usually leaning against fences, railings, hedges and kerbs. Others lay about on the banks. People sat chatting on bikes. For much of the year you would seldom be fishing for long without talking to somebody

124

on a bike. In the evenings or at week-ends our non-fishing friends turned up on their bikes to talk.

We talked about favourite radio programmes (particularly Tommy Handley's ITMA), about films (especially the Marx Brothers, Bing Crosby, Bob Hope and Dorothy Lamour) or about the latest war news. Sometimes a whole radio programme or film would be described in detail so that, even if you hadn't heard or seen it, you would finish up by knowing all about it. Jokes were always included.

One evacuee who came most evenings was Mo Miller. He had as strong an interest in aeroplanes as I had in fish, and when there were only the two of us our talk took the form of a quiz: he asked me a question about planes, and I asked him one about fish or fishing. Such was the specialist nature of our questions that we often went weeks without one of us being able to answer a single question of the other's.

We were mostly boys, so it wasn't surprising that our conversations were often about girls. More interesting was that some girls used to come to the Long Pond also; not to fish, but to talk. A lot of the talk was on the same lines as the conversations between boys, but the girls brought a very different point of view about fishing. They were against it. Their basic argument was simple: it was cruel. Anglers hook fish, which must inflict intense pain. Then the fish were taken out of their water, and this caused pain too. In addition to that, anglers frightened fish in all sorts of ways. How would we like to be hooked, and held under water?

We argued that we *liked* fish. We hurt them as little as possible, and always put them back. We liked to see them in their natural habitat, and were often happy enough simply to know they were there. We read about them, learnt about them and took an interest in them that most other people didn't. If it wasn't for us, very few people would know they were there at all. Some local people had no idea what the Long Pond and surrounding waters held. And anglers formed movements like the Pure Rivers Society to prevent fish being poisoned.

The girls argued that if we really liked fish we wouldn't hurt or frighten them, and would be happy enough to watch them or just to know they were there. We agreed with the girls on some points. We thought it was cruel for deep sea fishermen to catch fish and let them die in their thousands out of water. But that didn't prevent us from arguing also that fish was a necessary food, and we were always on the look-out for examples of tribes whose staple diet was fish - because not much else was available. In such parts of the world people respected fish, even worshipped them, and fish were a part of their culture just as cattle and chickens were part of ours. But the girls were consistent: catching fish was cruel because they suffered pain, even if people did need to eat fish to keep alive.

I found these differences of opinion fascinating. On the one side were

125

these girls who had practically nothing to do with fish. They didn't go around looking at every small bit of water, wanting to see what was there. They didn't read about fish, and knew little about them. They didn't know the excitement of fish - how even a picture on a tin of sardines was interesting. They didn't realise how, every time we saw a fish in the water, whether big 'un or tiddler, we were glad it was there, and felt an affinity with it. Yet the girls were arguing against cruelty, and we boys were defending it! I had, at one time, kissed the fish I caught and wanted to tell them I was their friend. The girls would probably think it stupid to kiss fish (I never told them about it), yet they wouldn't hurt them in the first place.

Some of the girls come for a chat at the Lines

At the level of discussion we had, the girls were clearly more consistent and rational. In fact their arguments pre-dated by over half a century the views of today's animal rights, welfare and liberation movements. (See for example *Animal Liberation* by Peter Singer - Pimlico)

None of us changed our views at the time, but perhaps we influenced one another's later thinking.

Hedgelaying

One of our most enjoyable games couldn't really be practised at the Long Pond, but we often spent whole days at it and were still playing it years after the war had ended. We called it hedgelaying.

It was nothing like the agricultural activity of laying a hedge. In fact it should more properly be called 'hedge-lying' because it finished with someone

126

lying in a hedge. We would select a hedge that had no barbed wire or posts in it then, having carefully worked out a route, would take a run and jump right into it, usually turning in mid-air and landing backwards.

The game of hedgelaying received a fillip whenever large areas of allotments had to be abandoned for development. Men who had patiently and energetically cultivated allotments most of their lives, and been highly praised during the war for doing so, had their plots taken from them. A good deal of sadness and ill feeling resulted. One allotment-holder near Mill Houses, having been told he would have to leave, one day retired to his old shed and was found dead there. Mr Peckover claimed he had died of a broken heart.

There were two allotment areas on the marshes that were left uncultivated for a long time before they were finally built on. Almost every plot was surrounded by well-tended hedges about four feet high, and we could jump, roll or even dive head first into them. We would start at one end of the allotments and go along miles of hedge. Some of the allotment gardens were almost like a maze, and it took hours to go round them. Strangely, it didn't damage the hedges much at all, partly because they recovered quickly, partly because there was so much length of hedge, and partly because we hardly ever jumped in the same place twice. There were variations on the normal jump - like giving someone a leg-up when he took off. Sometimes several of us would pick up a player by the arms and legs and throw him up into the hedge. We had to be careful not to go right over the hedge and land on the other side, but that was the only danger.

It was Robert Rose's favourite game and, nearly sixty years later, he'd still like to try it. But he doesn't see many hedges these days.

Brief Call

'Caught any?'

The question was put in a northern accent by a soldier in the King's Royal Rifles. He had several rods, a landing-net handle and a rodrest all tied together, and carried a large creel over his shoulder. Soldiers occasionally watched us fishing at the Long Pond, but this was one of the few who ever came to fish.

'I've got one,' I replied.

I was fishing between numbers 3 and 4 in Harecroft Parade, near the Point. The soldier put his creel down on the grass only a few yards away.

'What was it?'

I lifted out my keep-net and showed him a 4-lb carp. He looked surprised.

'That big here, are they?'

'They go a lot bigger,' I said. 'Some 15- to 20-pounders.'

He whistled, and began quickly fitting together a 3-joint split cane rod. He had just taken an expensive-looking reel from his creel when, glancing up, he saw 19-year-old Colleen looking down at him from the upstairs window of number 3 - a house also called 'Colleen'.

The soldier paused. Then, instead of fitting his reel on to the rod, he lifted it up to his mouth.

'Hello! Anyone at home?' He put the reel to his ear. Colleen smiled down:

'Yes, I'm in.'

The soldier put the reel to his mouth again. 'Are you married?' The reel went back to his ear. Colleen replied:

'Not yet.'

The reel went again to the soldier's mouth. 'Feel like a chat over the phone?' The reel went back to his ear again.

Colleen replied: 'I don't mind, especially with someone like you at the other end.'

There were chuckles from some boys fishing towards the Boards. It was such a typical Colleen remark. But she couldn't have been expecting what followed. The soldier proceeded to tell her he had been billeted near the station for three days, he was twenty-three, born in Yorkshire, worked in the textile trade and lived with his parents until called up. He was a keen angler, as was his father, and they had fished most of the well-known waters in northern England. He told Colleen how old his parents were, what they did for a living, about the family cat, about relatives, where he went to school, about army life, and that he was expecting to go abroad at any moment. He occasionally lifted the reel to his ear, or asked a question, but most of the time he was telling Colleen all about himself. Colleen was happy to let him go on, and he talked for over two hours by which time the street lights had come on.

Eventually there was a call from inside the house: 'Colleen!'

The soldier peered at his watch. 'By the centre! I'm supposed to be back!'

Colleen said: 'Nice to have had a chat,' and disappeared from view.

The soldier put his reel back into the creel, dismantled his rod, slipped it into its bag, tied rods, landing-net handle and rod-rest together, and set off rapidly towards the Loke. I wondered if he realised the quickest way back to the station was in the opposite direction.

While he had been talking I had caught two more carp, both rather larger than the four-pounder he had seen. He must have known I caught them because I had made a lot more fuss than necessary when playing them. But he hadn't paused in his life history. He had been looking up at Colleen all the time, and hardly glanced towards the water.

He never reappeared on the banks of the Long Pond. Perhaps he went abroad a day or two later.

And I have often wondered how he knew there was a pond there at all.

Long Pond Characters

There were not many young men who fished in the Long Pond and as the war progressed they became even fewer. But we did have two role models for a time before they disappeared, probably called up for military service.

John Bunn was a burly man in his early twenties and always in shirt sleeves. He lived in Harewood Parade, so could see the Long Pond from his window. If you saw a green and white float with a balsa-wood bowl and thin cane stem, you could be almost sure he had made it. If ever we needed a rod-ring tied on, or something mended, he would always be willing to do it for us. He fished most often in the Long Pond, almost directly in front of where he lived.

Don Foreman was only about eighteen or nineteen, and always immaculately dressed even when fishing. He lived in the end house along Kettlewell Lane, so could fish in the Side of Leccy from his own garden. He would stand a yard or two from his front door, almost directly above where the water poured in from the Saunders, and let his float trot fifteen feet below with the current until it was almost out of sight the other side of the corrugated iron fence. The only other place he fished was the Saunders itself. He always sat on the side of the flotsam bin, cast out as near the dam as he could by the back of the last house in Archdale Street, and let his tackle go with the current until it was almost level with the back of the last house in Eastgate Street. He usually had a fish, or at least a bite, every five casts or so. He mostly caught roach of up to a quarter of a pound. I never knew him to fish in the Long Pond. If you saw a float similar to those of John Bunn, but coloured green and red, you could be almost certain Don had made it.

John and Don were usually together, making or repairing tackle, talking about fish and fishing and making aquaria. By about the autumn of 1940 they had both disappeared, and I never saw either of them again.

Don Foreman and John Bunn were the first adults I knew at the Long Pond, but the earliest I heard about were the Dutchmen. They used to come to the pond with 'canes as long as half the width of the pond'. For a long time I assumed they must have had canes like mine, but longer. But they probably had jointed roach poles. They had been the immigrants who lived along the River Ouse near The Point and were engaged on maintaining the river banks. One person who remembered the Dutchmen was old Mr Spinks. He always came fishing dressed in suit and waistcoat, cap and polished shoes. He had a heavy, spirally-bound rod, always fished with worm, and always in the same place - a yard from the Point, towards the railway. I only ever knew him to catch eels. Mr Spinks was old enough to have grandsons, one of whom was a young angler.

Mr Pegg was probably in his early forties at the start of the war. He had a split cane rod, and was the first we ever knew to use a fixed-spool reel - an

Alcock Stanley. He maintained that fixed-spool reels would never replace pin-reels because they kinked your line. He liked fishing in the Lily Pond, and was more often there than at the Long Pond. He fished very fine, yet still managed to land good carp in spite of the lilies. Having landed a four-pound carp in the Lily Pond one day, he was removing the hook when a boy asked if he could have it. Mr Pegg looked up.

'What do you want it for?'

'For my cat,' replied the boy.

Mr Pegg frowned. 'Fish are more important than bloody cats!' With that he put the fish back into the Lily Pond.

The Lily Pond side in wartime

Mr Pegg did a lot of fishing also at the Horseshoe Pond along Estuary Road which was then in open countryside. The Horseshoe held various kinds of fish including carp, and Mr Pegg often told me of those he had caught there. It was a quiet place, frequented by herons. Sometimes they caught eels and either ate them there, or flew off with them. The Horseshoe sounded a nice place but, probably because we found the Long Pond so wonderful, most of us never fished there.

Tom Mitchley lived in Loke Road, almost opposite the pond. He knew all about fish and fishing, and could recognise the make of a rod from a distance of twenty yards. He always appeared as soon as a big fish was hooked, yet never once did we know him to come fishing.

Butch Greef was about my own age, and often spent a lot of time at the pond - but not to fish. His main interest was in stone-throwing, and we had many long contests seeing who could first hit objects we perched high up on the sides of railway trucks. I missed many a bite at the railway end of the pond and in the Square because of our contests.

One boy I never knew to fish was Chunky. He could play a tune by cupping his hands and clapping them in front of his mouth - which he shaped to produce any particular note. It was a fascinating technique. Chunky was quite willing to teach me how to do it, and I wanted to learn. Years later I taught my own sons to do it. I still play tunes Chunky's way, and never do so without thinking of him.

Toddy was in his twenties when we first knew him at the Long Pond. He always fished at the railway end by the tunnel, usually throwing his bait by hand as far under the tunnel as he could get. He liked fishing at night, and stood a torch, lamp or candle on the ledge just above the water to illuminate his float. When Toddy met someone for the first time he always asked:

'How much do you think I weigh?'

When he asked me this question I didn't know how to answer. Should I over- or under-estimate? I gave what I thought was a fair guess, and Toddy grinned.

'Ha! There's something you don't know! I weigh less than you think because I've only got one foot.'

Toddy had been a promising soccer player until losing a foot in an accident, but he still managed to cycle to the pond from where he lived in Gaywood. He already had several children, and one of the reasons he gave for coming fishing was to get away from family duties.

Although young, Toddy spoke a lot of old Norfolk, saying things like: 'Accordingly to him he caught three carp yesterday,' or: 'I skun the eel and eat it.'

Toddy was fond of a chat, and never seemed to worry about disturbing the fish. He could talk for hours on all kinds of subjects - including sex. He knew all the rougher characters of the neighbourhood whom we avoided. Late one evening he was standing with some of them on Highgate Bridge when one notorious character picked up one of the crowd and held him, with one hand, over the parapet twenty feet above the water. All the unfortunate victim could do was plead:

'Now don't do it, Tom, don't do it!'

Toddy would often get someone to go and buy chips for him, both for eating and for bait. Once, he was leaning against the rails talking and eating chips when a young lady came walking from the Loke direction. In the middle of a story Toddy nonchalantly flicked a chip towards the lady, hitting her in the eye. It must have hurt, and she was unable to see for a while. When she had recovered somewhat she exclaimed:

131

'You ruffian! I've a good mind to smack your face!'

She didn't, but as she made her way through the first kissing-gate Toddy said: 'Ah! I b'lieve you would an all!'

We young anglers would see some people go past four times a day as they went off to work, came home at midday, went off to work again, and came home when they had finished for the day. A lot of these knew practically nothing about the fish that were in the pond, and were surprised to see even a half-pounder caught. Some people, passing the pond at night when nobody else was about, were frightened out of their wits by the huge splashes that some of the larger fish made. One of the passers-by who did know about the fish was Mr Sainty, a chimney sweep. He walked very slowly, hands behind his back, so was visible for a long time as he was coming and as he was going. He went out in the morning, and came back at midday. Then he went off again at about one o'clock in the afternoon, and reappeared about six. In the evening he went past again from the Loke and through the kissing-gates. Finally, he appeared some time after eleven o'clock at night, still with hands behind his back, and walking rather less steadily. Mr Sainty always went round the pond in a clockwise direction; coming from the Loke he went by Harewood Parade, and coming from the kissing-gate, towards the Loke, he always took Harecroft Parade. The only time Sainty spoke was on his way home at night, and then only to one person: Neville Tunmore. He would ask:

'What have you caught, then?'

Neville would either describe what he had caught or, if he had the fish in his keep-net he would pull that up and show Mr Sainty the fish. But if Neville had to admit to having caught nothing, Sainty would always say:

'You want to put chocolate in that bait.'

Christopher Tunmore, Neville's younger brother, was usually having some adventure or other. He found fireworks, especially 'penny dreadfuls', fascinating and would often 'tempt' the fuse with a match, withdrawing the flame at the last fraction of a second so the firework didn't actually go off. He was doing this indoors in the lounge one day when he miscalculated and the fuse began to fizz. He rushed to the window, opened it, and threw the firework hard towards the pond. But just as he threw, the window blew shut, and the firework bounced off the glass, into the room and under the table. He scrambled on to the floor, grabbed the firework, and had time only to throw it into the fireplace. The deafening explosion echoed in the chimney and a huge amount of soot fell down covering the grate and billowing all over the room. Fortunately his parents were out at the time, and he was able to spend several hours taking buckets of soot out on to the railway embankment and cleaning the room. Only a few days later Mr Sainty called to do the chimneys, and as he left he said to Mrs Tunmore:

'Your husband said that one in the lounge hadn't been done for years, and was all blocked up, but there was hardly anything in it.'

The Tunmores' bath was often full of quarter-pound roach, all as lively as if they were in the Gaywood River. It made me think of my own efforts at keeping fish in the old copper, and I asked Chris how he managed it. Apparently he fed them a lot of his own meals, and replenished the bath from the Long Pond every few hours.

As a young angler Chris was surprisingly successful, and caught a lot of big 'uns. One of his favourite places was under the Swan Laundry bridge. He would sit with his back to Highgate School and fish as far under the bridge as he could get. There he caught carp, roach, bream and, occasionally, a perch or tench. One night he was fishing there in pitch darkness when he caught something. As soon as he felt it he said:

'Hello! What's this?'

When he got it to the side, and put the landing net under it, he was vaguely aware of a shape running round the landing-net ring. He said:

'Hello! What's this?' Then he saw something moving up the landing-net handle. 'Hello! What's this?'

In no time at all the something was over his hand and running up his arm. 'Hello! What's this?'

Then it was on to his shoulder and jumped off on to the bank behind. This time he said: 'Hello! What was that?'

I was never sure what it was, and I don't think he ever found out.

Old Ken

We called him 'Old Ken' although he was probably only in his forties. He worked on the land, always wore a cap, was only slightly-built but had enormous hands with freckles. He was a bachelor, and had lodgings in Smith Avenue. He often fished in the Lily Pond with his short rod, very heavy line and a large, eyed hook tied to the end. He always fished with worm and we thought he would only ever catch eels. He did catch eels, but also got carp, roach, bream, tench, rudd and, once, a chub.

At that time there were lots of small ponds dotted all over West Norfolk, and we occasionally cycled off to fish outside Lynn. One regular place was Tottenhill where there were small ponds holding tench. It was interesting to go elsewhere sometimes because we always came back realising how lucky we were to have the Long Pond. We didn't go very often, but when we did go, as often as not we set out on our bikes with no particular destination in mind. We just went looking for water, and as far as I remember we always found somewhere to fish.

One day Old Ken and I set out through South Lynn and off in the Wisbech direction. After some miles we noticed a clump of bushes and trees some way off the road, so went to investigate. We fought our way through

brambles and sinky mud and arrived at a small pond only about thirty feet across, with a depth of four to five feet. The water was absolutely clear, but we could see nothing moving, and the place looked dead. We were about to go back to the bikes when a huge eel emerged from just below where we were standing and swam slowly away, keeping to the bottom. It was the biggest eel I had ever seen. When it reached the middle it seemed to falter and turn its head round slightly. Then it continued, and went out of sight under overhanging branches on the other side.

Old Ken fishing from Side of Leccy with Back of Leccy willows visible

As the enormous eel had paused, and half turned, I had the strong impression that it had looked back in reproach, as if asking us to go away and leave it in peace. I felt guilty. What right had we to come here and disturb that creature? Here it was, in a pond that didn't seem to have been visited by anyone for a long time, and we had come with our fishing tackle trying to get it out. Such an eel would soon want to be off overland to find a river, the sea and then the Sargasso. Old Ken was an eel enthusiast and I was sure he would be tempted to try and catch it. I moved back quietly and, to my surprise, Old Ken did the same. I led the way to our bikes, hardly able to believe that my friend was following. When we got to the bikes I said:

'Shall we go on a bit to see what else there is?'

Old Ken mumbled agreement and we got on our bikes. I pedalled fast in case Old Ken should change his mind.

Later, as we were eating our sandwiches, Ken said:

'You didn't mind about that eel, did you?' I said I didn't mind, and tried to change the subject in case he had thought of going back there. But to my surprise he said:

'I had a funny feeling about that great eel. I thought it looked round at us and asked us to go away.'

I have often wondered what that eel weighed. We both thought it must have been over three feet long and nearly three inches thick. At the end of the day we had caught very little, but we were both glad we hadn't caught the eel.

One Saturday morning I called on Old Ken in Smith Avenue to see if he wanted to come out looking for a pond or two. An hour later we were cycling through South Wootton with fishing gear and sandwiches, and were soon going along a narrow road in Norfolk heathland. Some eight or ten miles from Lynn we saw a path off to the left, took that and soon almost stepped into a small pond. It was typical of the area: circular, not much more than fifteen feet across, and surrounded by bracken. There were water lilies, but clear spaces to fish in. There were thousands and thousands of flies about, all over our faces and hands, and in our hair. Once, looking above me I saw a column of flies so high that I nearly lost my nerve and ran off. Even Old Ken was finding it hard going. We had caught one or two small tench when Old Ken decided to move to the other side. He lifted up his folding stool to reveal an adder, head up and partly coiled. It didn't move as Ken went over to the other side, and didn't disappear for a minute or two. Not long after that, Old Ken found another under his bag. I jumped up to find I had been almost sitting on yet another adder. We returned the three or four small tench and set off at a run, trying to get away from the columns of flies above our heads. We didn't manage this until on our bikes again, pedalling as fast as we could. Further on we took another narrow lane, went past a house, and came to a much bigger pond. It was obvious that people fished there because several places on the banks were worn, and some places had been cleared of lilies. There were far fewer flies, and we could see there were no adders in the shortish grass.

Later in the afternoon a couple of small boys came along and told us that there were tench and good rudd in the pond. We had caught some of both, but nothing over half a pound. Then another boy arrived, about my own age, and stood on the opposite bank looking over at us. When the two younger boys went off, he threw some stones into the water just in front of them, and laughed. The two boys weren't out of sight when a cat came up on the other side. It was black, and looked about half-grown. The boy looked down, saw the cat, immediately picked it up and hurled it right into the middle of the pond. He threw it with one hand, and the poor cat was in the air for several seconds. It hit the surface, went under water, reappeared and struck out for the side, doing what I can only describe as a strong crawl. It swam holding its head high out of the water, and went fast through open water and lilies alike. It reached the bank and ran into the bracken. It was the only time I have seen a cat swim. I reeled in, and walked round the pond as though looking for a different place. Behind the boy, I dropped my rod, grabbed him round the neck and wrestled him into the pond. I was up to my thighs in mud and water, but I had the boy in a headlock and he couldn't do anything except thrash about helplessly. I held his head under for as long as I dared, gave him a push, clambered out, grabbed my rod and bag and got to my bike. I shouted:

'Come on Ken!'

Old Ken was close behind me as I cycled off along the lane. We passed the house and, on impulse, instead of turning left towards Lynn I turned right. We pedalled as fast as we could, our rods waving about over the road. I was dripping water from the waist down, leaving a trail behind us. I shouted:

'Did he get out, Ken?'

Ken said: 'Ah! But we might have the family after us!'

We saw a road to the left, and took it. A few minutes later we stopped, quickly dismantled our rods and packed tackle away. I feverishly squeezed as much water from trousers and socks as possible and we set off again. With rods tied to our handlebars, and hardly any trail of water left, we felt safer. We returned to Lynn by a roundabout route expecting at each junction to be stopped by a family bent on vengeance, or even by the police. But nobody waylaid us. If there had been any pursuers, perhaps they had kept going northwards, thinking we were heading for Hunstanton.

I told Mrs Peckover I had fallen in because of an adder. Perhaps the other boy told his parents he had fallen in. We wondered if the cat had ever been thrown in before. Its lack of suspicion as it stood near the boy suggested it hadn't. I only hoped it was never thrown in again.

Ponded!

Before ever daring to fish in the Long Pond I often walked past to see what was happening. One day I stopped to watch two young men, about eighteen or nineteen, who were fishing directly opposite what I later knew to be the Tunmores' house. A man in his early twenties came up on a bike carrying a rod and creel, stopped, leant the bike against the railings and took out a reel.

'What'll you give me for this?'

The two others watched as he flicked the reel, making it spin, demonstrated an effective ratchet and showed how much line there was on it. The reel looked new. It was made of bakelite and about six inches in diameter. There was no offer.

'Come on! How much?' The other two shook their heads.

'I'll take five shillings for it!'

One of the others raised his eyebrows. 'I bet you will.'

'All right, four shillings.' It was a wonderful reel and I regretted not having four shillings. 'Give me half a crown.' The others were still not interested. 'A shilling then!'

But still the others weren't interested.

'Right! Give me sixpence for it or I'll chuck it in the pond!'

I thought I might scrape together sixpence myself if I could borrow half of that from my hosts, but the man was looking angry and had taken no notice of me.

'Sixpence or I chuck it!'

The others still said nothing whereupon the man hurled that beautiful reel right out into the middle, got on to his bike and pedalled furiously away. It was the first thing I had seen thrown into the Long Pond.

Not many days after starting to fish at the Long Pond I noticed a splash two-thirds of the way out from the Boards. It hadn't looked like a fish jumping, but I kept an eye on the spot just in case. Then I saw what looked like roots, vegetation and soil rise up from the garden opposite, sail over the hedge, path, railings and anglers to land with another splash. I asked one of the boys fishing nearby who was doing the throwing. He rolled his eyes:

'That's old Nicholas. He's always throwing rubbish in.'

Mr Nicholas's house was on the corner of Loke Road and Harecroft Parade, and his garden went a quarter of the way along the pond on that side. Unfortunately the man was a keen gardener who got rid of his weeds and other garden refuse by simply throwing it over the hedge and into the pond. As the weeks and months went by, and he still threw garden rubbish in, I half expected to see an island appear.

Sometimes, as clumps sailed over anglers' heads, and landed near floats, there would be a shout of:

'Hoi!'

But the man was never deterred, and used the pond as a dump for years. He was some kind of policeman, so that was perhaps why anglers didn't complain more vehemently.

Garden rubbish was an exception. Usually it was things like stones or bricks. But we dredged out other things: bike wheels, push chairs, tyres or pieces of timber. Sometimes these objects were in deep water, out of sight, and we first knew about them through getting hooked up on them. Occasionally we did a special dredging operation over the whole pond, ending up with a large pile of rubbish that we then had to dispose of, and this we did by taking it far enough away not to be a temptation to throw it in again.

The main snags in the Lily Pond were, of course, the lilies themselves which were cut once a year by council men. In later years the council had the Long Pond side dredged once or twice, and this left a greater depth with no snags. But only days after one of these clear-outs I saw two objects just below the surface near the railway end. I managed to get out what proved to be an old wheelbarrow. The two objects had been the handles.

The easiest thing to throw in was a stone. Sometimes there would be a splash near your float followed by rapidly retreating steps towards the Loke or railway. But bearing in mind how many people went past the pond each day, there was very little stone-throwing. The biggest menace, especially during the first half of the war, was Gerard Bunn. He lived in Harewood Parade, and was the nephew of our friend John Bunn who had by that time left the Long Pond scene. Gerard used to collect a supply of stones from his garden, and bombard all the floats he could reach. We were always trying to catch him, but he made sure he kept near enough to his house to be able to reach it before we caught up with him. Although young, he could judge distances to a foot, and time to a fraction of a second. We sometimes tried to distract his attention so one of us could creep up between him and his house, but we never managed it. His technique was foolproof.

More than once a frustrated angler, having just missed catching Gerard, knocked on his door and complained to his mother. She always maintained her son wouldn't throw stones. Once or twice she called him to the door to confront the complainant.

'Gerard, have you been throwing stones?'

He always denied it, and his mother always believed him. His stone-throwing usually frightened the fish off for half an hour, and that wouldn't have been so bad, but the trouble was he tended to do it every half hour.

Later, Gerard became a young angler himself. At an early age he had expensive tackle, and fished fine, often catching more than his peers who fished with canes and bent pins. He was fond of shouting 'Garim!' before he had in fact 'got' a fish, which was annoying. Even more annoying was that he usually had 'Garim!' But even after becoming an angler he continued his stone-throwing when not fishing himself. Nearly sixty years later Neville Tunmore still regrets not having been able to catch Gerard. When he moved away, the Long Pond was a much more peaceful place.

One day the Kendall brothers, some other Lynn boys and I were fishing together between the Boards and the Point. Suddenly the elder of the Kendalls said:

'Look out! Here comes trouble.'

Seconds later a hail of stones hit the water amongst our floats. The thrower, a boy of about my own age, was standing opposite, making no attempt to run off or hide. He threw a few more stones, as hard as he could, then scrabbled about at the bottom of Mr Nicholas' hedge looking for more. He threw these into the water just in front of us. The younger Kendall told me, in a whisper, that the boy lived along Turbus Road and was always fighting. The boy went off to the Lily Pond, and we thought he had gone. But he soon appeared again, carrying more stones, threw some from the Loke pavement, then came up behind us. He threw a few more over our heads into the pond, then came right down the bank to where we were standing and began shying at our floats from there. At any moment he was surely going to hit one of our floats and ruin it.

The elder Kendall brother looked at me and said:

'Stop him, Reg!'

I was wary of doing anything but, when my float had been missed by inches I said:

'OK mate, you'd better run away or you'll feel my fist in your face!'

He threw two or three more stones, having taken no notice at all of me. I went up to him.

'If you throw one more stone I'll bash you up!'

He felt in a pocket, produced a stone, and threw it into the water. He seemed unworried, which made me feel nervous. If he was always fighting perhaps he was very good at it. Perhaps his father was a boxer and had

138

coached him. But I had gone too far to back out now. I moved away up the bank on to the road, saying:

'Right! You come over here!'

At the top of the bank I put my fists up. I'd have been happy if the boy had run off at that point, but he didn't. To my dismay he came up the bank and raised his own fists.

I did the only thing I could and flew at him, both fists flying. He had to move back to avoid being hit, and was unable to get a punch in himself. Encouraged, I kept up the furious barrage of punches. He backed away further, as far as Loke Road. I kept flailing away as he retreated over the road, skipping backwards all the time. We went along the side of the Lily Pond towards Smith Avenue, and I was wondering how long I could keep it up. Then, when we reached Smith Avenue, the boy turned and fled towards Peck's Field. I had hardly landed a proper blow, but that didn't matter. We had got rid of him, at least for the moment. As I turned back, the others were standing on the Loke pavement, cheering. I took my time walking back because I didn't want to appear too out of breath and, by the time I reached the pond, the others had all formed themselves into pairs. One of each pair pretended to throw a stone in the water, the other said:

'Right! You come over here!'

Then they both moved to the top of the bank, and the stone-thrower was put to flight by the flailing fists of the other one. They could hardly do it for laughing. For some weeks after that I was known as:

'Right-you-come-over-here-Reg.'

Fortunately I was never called upon to live up to the reputation I had acquired in those few seconds.

•••╫╟╫╢╫╟╫••••

For many years a huge advertisement board stood on two heavy posts by the railings at the Loke Road end of the Long Pond. It was the property of the London and North Eastern Railway company. One day it fell down and was promptly appropriated by Neville Tunmore and Joseph Pegg. They decided to make a raft out of it, and go sailing in the pond. It would easily take two boys. They worked on it regularly and carefully for weeks, watched with interest by Mr Tunmore - who even made one or two suggestions for its conversion. When it was ready, and the boys announced it was to be launched, Mr Tunmore refused to allow it on the water. The boys were of course disappointed, and Neville was also furious. Probably his father hadn't realised the possible dangers until the last minute. That raft must have been one of the biggest things the Long Pond was ever threatened with.

•••╫╟╫╢╫╟╫••••

Fred Remington

Fred Remington lived at number four, Harecroft Parade, by the Point. He would often come out of his house with plates, and scrape the left-overs into the pond. We thought it attracted carp, because that was a very good place for the big 'uns. When he retired, his main hobby was going 'Down Below' (going out fishing in a boat from the Fisher Fleet). Whenever he returned from the Fisher Fleet he would bring a net of shrimps with him, and what he didn't eat he took out in his net and hurled into the pond. It was excellent ground bait, and if you fished from the Point with a shrimp, especially one of his, you stood a good chance of catching a carp.

One day Mr Tunmore arrived home to find a crowd and a fire engine by his gate. Firemen were packing equipment away, and said they had used pond water to put out a fire on the railway embankment next to the Tunmores' garden. When the fire brigade had left, Mr Tunmore tried to discover how the fire had started. His wife said the grass was very dry and would easily catch fire, but he wasn't satisfied. Christopher's most treasured possession was a six-inch diameter lens which both he and Neville used for examining tiny insects. They also sometimes held it up to the sun and set light to things. Mr Tunmore finally got an admission from Neville who, in his defence, claimed he had been looking at insects for hours, and focused on a dead leaf for only a few seconds.

'So you set light to the embankment with that lens, did you?' roared the father. 'Right! I'll pond it!'

He was taking the lens outside when Christopher came home and claimed it wasn't fair. It was his lens, he hadn't set light to the embankment, and Neville didn't have his permission to use it. With the help of his mother, Christopher managed to persuade his father not to throw the lens into the pond. Reluctantly Mr Tunmore returned the lens.

'All right! But any more trouble and I'll pond it!'

Some weeks later the Tunmores were sitting down at the table when Mr Tunmore said:

'Funny about that post.' Nobody said anything. Mr Tunmore went on: 'You know. The one near the shed. I couldn't see it from the kitchen.'

Some time after the meal Mr Tunmore came storming indoors.

'Do you think I don't know my own garden? Where's that lens? I'll pond it now!'

140

The post in question had been heavily creosoted, and Christopher had not been able to resist the temptation to put a lighted match on the top of it. By the time he and his mother had managed to put the flames out half the post had burnt away. Mr Tunmore usually carried out his threats, but on that occasion his wife argued strongly that the lens hadn't been used, and that it was a very educational toy. What with this argument and Christopher's tears, Mr Tunmore finally relented.

'But if ever anything is set light to again around here, that lens will be ponded! Is that clear?' Christopher assured his father that he understood.

One afternoon, some time later, Christopher was roaming around the house with his lens, wondering how he could use it. He went into the lounge where his father was asleep in an armchair. On the arm of the chair was a packet of cigarettes and a box of matches. Christopher thought he would puzzle his father by making a burn mark on the matchbox. He would never guess it had been done with the lens . Christopher held the lens in the sun and focused on the matchbox.

There was no warning. The matchbox exploded and burning matches flew all over the room.

Mr Tunmore had been in the first world war, very young, and still had terrible nightmares about his war experiences. He often screamed in the night, thrashed about and fell out of bed. He awoke now with a shriek and saw matches burning on the table, the floor and in his lap. He jumped up, put out the burning matches and grabbed the lens.

'This time it *will* be ponded!'

He stormed out through the front door and, from the grass bank where most of the games took place, hurled the lens into the pond. It landed within inches of that bakelite reel.

Bottomless Well

I was cycling back towards Lynn, not far from Pott Row, when there came a glint of water from my left. I stopped, turned back and looked through the hedge. It was a pond that came up to within a few feet of the road. It looked deep. There was a gate further along so I climbed over it into a field and got to the other side of the pond. It was about 25 yards long and 15 wide, with water lilies over some of the surface. In one place the bank was slightly worn as if someone might occasionally fish there.

Within a week I was back there with a rod, fishing from the field. The first time I caught some rudd and two tench - the largest about three pounds. I visited that pond until many years after the war. At one period there were two brothers aged about 5 and 8 who also fished there. They lived in a house only fifty yards away, and when they knew I was there they would come running over the field to join me. They caught a lot of fish, and talked about 'fat ol' tench' with enthusiasm. When I asked if they knew the depth of the pond they said it had a 'bottomless well'. I was only too happy to go along with this idea.

'Bottomless well' at Leziate - now 'only a large hole'

The last time I saw that pond was when Neville took me on his Triumph Terrier motor-bike - a bit of a let-down after having always cycled there. It drizzled all day and when we packed up the motor-bike refused to start. We tried to coax it into life for some time, but had to return to Lynn under our own steam. Neville sat at the front, guiding, while I sat behind and punted with my landing net handle. It was all right on the flat, and downhill, but to go uphill I had to get off and push. The landing net handle was only cane, but it stood up well to the six-mile test, suffering only a slightly worn end, and a permanent bend.

I last visited the place in the early 1990s with a friend who had worked for the National Rivers Authority. We went into the field to find only a large hole where the pond had been. We stood in the lowest part and calculated we were eleven feet below what had been the water level. Not a 'bottomless well', but a good depth for a small pond. The water table had gone down more than eleven feet. Peat shrinkage has also happened there, and what was a beautiful wet area now needs huge watering machines to get crops growing. It was a sad sight, and we didn't stay long.

142

Neville Tunmore

Neville Tunmore and David Curston were traction engine enthusiasts and at one time spent ages building a working model. They could often be seen carrying the partly-built engine past the pond between each other's houses, or taking it off to the allotment for testing. They spent weeks carefully making and fitting one small part. One day Neville was fishing at the Loke Road end of the pond, opposite the Boards, when his attention was attracted by a familiar noise. It was a traction engine coming along the Loke. It slowed and stopped level with him. The driver got down and walked towards Neville.

'What sort of water is this?'

'Pardon?'

'I mean is it fresh water? Or salt?'

'Oh! It's fresh water.'

The driver returned to his engine, unwound a pipe, put the end into the pond and began pumping water into the traction engine's tank. After a while he stopped the pumping, removed the pipe and stowed it away. He thanked Neville and drove off.

••••••

I had been fishing at the Boards without success and was going to try at the Point. I had just reached the turning circle when there came a whooshing sound from the other end. I looked up to see a jet of water about fifteen feet high rising from the pond just the other side of the Tunmores' house. It died down almost immediately and I could see Neville standing on the bank next to where the jet had been. As I ran up he was still staring around him.

'It went on my head!'

It was the only water spout we ever knew at the pond.

••••••

Dick, one of Mr Peckover's brothers emigrated to the U.S.A. in the 1920s and didn't return to Britain until soon after the war when he retired to Florida. He and his wife spent a few days in Lynn, and I happened to be there at the same time. The first morning, Dick came up to me and held something out.

'This any good to you?'

It was a float, but not the sort we used in the Long Pond. It was made of red and white plastic, spherical and about one and a half inches in diameter, with a stem through the middle that worked on a spring. Dick said:

'Heard you've been interested in fishing for years. Got it in Florida.'

Since Dick had taken the trouble to bring it all the way from the U.S.A. I invited him along to the pond to see how it worked. With the Florida float

and a piece of boiled potato I cast out from the Boards. Dick said:
'That must be the first Florida float ever to be in the Long Pond.'

As usual one or two local residents came out for a chat, and at one point
Dick struck up a conversation with Mr Billman. Since there wasn't much
about in the way of bites I asked Mr Billman if he would keep an eye on the
float while I went off to find Neville so that Dick could meet him too. I went
past the Point and was level with the Tunmores' house when I saw the Florida
float not far from the railway end! A carp must have taken the potato as soon
as I left, and made a dash, overtaking me. It looked as if the fish had escaped
because the float wasn't moving. Then I noticed Neville on the concrete, right
at the end, fishing and talking to someone. I ran forward.

'Hey! Neville! Quick! Can you hook that Florida float out? There might
still be one on!'

Neville looked astonished. 'How did you know it was from Florida?'

It was then that I saw that the float, exactly the same as mine, was
attached to *Neville's* line.

Neville introduced me to his uncle who had emigrated to the U.S.A. in
the 1920s and recently retired to Florida. He was on a visit to see the family
and, knowing Neville was a keen angler, had brought him a float from that
part of the world. The floats were exactly the same in every respect, even
down to the colour. As far as we could work out we had all arrived at the
pond at the same time, and the two identical Florida floats must have hit the
water at more or less the same moment.

It was the first time we had ever seen such floats in the Long Pond and,
since they were not suitable for carp fishing, it wasn't surprising that we never
saw another.

*Neville Tunmore on the
turning circle near the Point*

Although surrounded by houses and roads,
and having the railway along one end, the
Long Pond still had a lot that was rural about
it. Apart from all the fish, birds, insects and
mammals that we had seen, we knew there
were also otters about. They seemed to prefer
the Gaywood River and we occasionally saw
the remains of a carp or roach there. We kept
it very quiet, and always buried or otherwise
disposed of the fish bones that were left on
banks. At one time there was an otter's holt
in the bank of the Long Pond not far from
the Point, but although we kept a close watch
we had never seen the otter itself. Then, one
night, Neville was fishing off the Boards and,

144

in the reflection of a street light, saw huge waves crossing the pond. He had heard no splash, so thought it might be an otter. Grabbing his torch, he ran as fast as he could to the other end of the pond, jumped the fence, flung himself down on to the concrete and shone his torch through the tunnel bars. The otter was crouching there, looking back at him.

⁜

Neville went fishing early one morning at the Lines. There was nobody about and it was quiet. From time to time large fish moved about, causing waves. It was a promising time and he expected a bite at any moment. Then a man came up, stopped on the bridge just by Neville's float, leant down and proceeded to rinse out a bucket. He splashed about for some minutes, clouding the water and causing a lot of disturbance. When the man finally went off Neville was prepared to give up and go elsewhere. But before the man was out of sight there were more waves and splashings than before. Neville had a bite, and caught a carp. Apparently the man had been coming to the same place at the same time every morning to clean his bucket out after feeding the poultry, and the fish had learnt to expect food at that time.

⁜

I once went along Harecroft Parade measuring how far each house was from the water. Number 1, the Tunmores', was closest and, as you went from Number 1 towards the Loke, houses were progressively further away. That was why the Long Pond cast was more effective at the Loke end.

From the very beginning of the war I was envious of Neville living in that house, yet at the time I didn't know the half of it. His room faced east and, early in the morning, the sun was reflected from the water's surface on to his ceiling. So he could lie in bed and, simply by looking up, tell whether the water was calm or, if there was a breeze, how much of a breeze. But wind patterns were different from the irregular movements caused by fish. When carp move about just below the surface they make large waves or ripples. So when a fish came near the surface, or broke the surface, there was a kaleidoscopic effect all over Neville's ceiling. He knew, without getting out of bed, what was happening in the Long Pond. Neville was often out early in the morning before any of us. For years we wondered how he managed it, not knowing that he had only to read his ceiling. What a wonderful house Number 1, Harecroft Parade was!

⁜

Neville had also noticed the filling-in of My Ditch and been appalled by it, but we didn't discover the mutual experience until well over half a century later.

145

To the Rescue

As early as my first day's fishing in the Long Pond a young angler had asked me to remove a hook for him. That was the first of hundreds of hooks I removed for anglers younger than I. When I was returning from school one day I saw Don Foreman fishing at the Saunders from the flotsam bin, and went over to watch. After a while he began rummaging in his bag.

'Here you are, Reg. You'll need this for some of those hooks you get out.'

It was a disgorger - my first. And it wasn't the most primitive sort with a V-shaped end. It was made of aluminium and had a slot into which you put the gut so as to follow it down to the hook. It made a lot of hook-removals much simpler and, I am sure, saved the lives of a lot of fish.

Removing hooks for others was the simple part. Persuading them to return the fish was often more difficult. Many young anglers wanted to take fish home to show their parents what they had caught, but they didn't have a bucket or even a jar to put them in. Some wanted to take fish away to give to their permanently hungry cat. Others wanted to keep the fish alive at home. When I removed a hook for someone, I argued that the fish wouldn't survive unless it was put back into the water immediately, that coarse fish were bad for cats and that fish couldn't be kept alive at home. If we were fishing from the Boards I would often point to the house opposite and remind the boy that the policeman who lived there always got to know if a fish had been taken away, and who had taken it, and that it was against the law. Sometimes I pointed to the gasping fish and tried to make the catcher feel pity. Later on I offered bribes: some line, a properly bent pin or an old hook to gut. Once I gave a boy a small, wooden reel for returning the fish. It was a constant battle. When I was removing a hook for someone else, I often cheated and let the fish slip back, pretending it was an accident.

One day a friend hooked a five-pound carp in the pond and had more or less played it out. I knew he intended to take the fish home, so made sure I was the one ready with a landing-net. Keeping myself between him and the fish I managed to get hold of the hook and remove it with one hand. The fish was gone in a flash and I pushed the hook into the landing-net meshes, pulling downwards on the net so that my friend thought the fish was still on. I jerked the net, making a splash, and groaned:

'He's off! Just about had him in the net, too.'

As he disentangled his hook from the mesh, my friend said:

'As you say, Reg, he must have been inside the net, so I'm going to claim him in my diary.' He did, so both of us were happy and so was the fish.

Later in the war I was passing the pond one evening and saw a carp of three to four pounds lying on the grass bank, flapping and gasping. Two men I had never seen before were fishing nearby. John, the elder Remington boy, was looking on and I asked him what was happening. One of the men had

146

caught the carp a few minutes before and intended to take it away. I went down the bank and stood, back to the water, admiring it. Then I picked it up.

'A good fish! Getting on for four pounds!' Then I pretended to slip backwards, landing on my bottom in the water, throwing the fish over my head into the middle of the pond. It must have looked quite convincing because one of the men laughed. The other one didn't look amused, neither was Mrs Peckover when I arrived home soaked to the skin.

Don Foreman's disgorger did excellent service for two years. Then one day I dropped it into the Back of Leccy and lost it. The next one I had lasted even longer. It was made of shiny metal, and had a slit all the way from top to bottom. You put the gut into the slit, then moved the disgorger downwards. I found it even more effective than the previous one. What was more it had a clip on it like a pen, so there was no need to keep it in a box, or loose in a pocket. After the war I used to spend a lot of time in Lynn. If it was only for a week-end I often cycled - on the Norfolk Giant. I was returning from one of these week-ends and decided to dismount and walk past the Eagle Pond in Snaresbrook. Half way along was a group of people standing on the bank and spilling out on to the road. From the edge of the crowd I could see three men holding down a swan, trying to remove a hook from its mouth. I stood my bike up and pushed to the front, removing the disgorger from my breast pocket. When I saw the swan's throat my heart sank. It was like a leather rasp, and the disgorger could only just reach as far as the hook. I struggled for some minutes but the hook wouldn't budge. I began sweating and, as time went on, became more and more desperate. In the end I decided the only thing to do was break the hook and hope the point would work its way out in time. I got the disgorger in position again and pushed hard. Nothing happened. It felt as if the disgorger would break before the hook. I shut my eyes and pushed blindly, hoping for the best. There was a snap, and I was amazed to see that the whole of the hook, including the barb, had come away, and that there was nothing apparently wrong with the swan's throat. The men put the bird back in the water and it swam strongly away. I pocketed the disgorger and staggered off. There was a spontaneous burst of clapping. I was too exhausted to point out that if it had been left to me the bird would probably not have had any help at all because I would never have dared to pick it up in the first place.

Cats

Dogs wandered everywhere in wartime Lynn, but there were quite a lot of cats about too. When I looked from the window along Loke Road we would see one run across every few minutes. It wasn't as dangerous for them then as it would be now because there was very little traffic, and a lot of that was horse-drawn or bicycles. The only private car ever parked along Loke Road belonged to Mr (Hungry) Fisher who lived between the Long Pond and Harecroft Gardens.

One local cat was Oscar who lived at Number 3, Harecroft Parade. He knew that people with rods and lines were likely suddenly to produce fish from the pond, and he would follow anglers around. When young anglers caught fish they would have to hold them high above the bank if they didn't want Oscar to jump up and get them first. It didn't take him long to dispose of a two-ouncer. It took him even less time to run off with one.

The local cat I knew best was Minnie, a half Persian tortoiseshell. She lived in the electric light works, and confined her activities almost entirely to the Side of Leccy, Back of Leccy and the Leccy Pit. When you arrived she rushed around, excited, allowing herself to be stroked, but anxious for you to get tackled up and begin. Once you were fishing she settled down beside you, staring out at your float. As soon as you hooked a fish, large or small, she would try to get at it. At the Leccy Pit she once got a fish into her mouth before it had been taken off the hook, and the angler, who had never met her before, had to rush to her, gathering in line as he went, and try to get her off. He didn't succeed, but did manage to get the hook out before Minnie swallowed it with the fish.

Minnie,
the electric light works cat

Another time, at the Back of Leccy, an angler caught a quarter-pound roach, but it dropped off into the grass. Minnie pounced, and was off, over the small plank bridge, into the generating station building.

My own approach with Minnie was to take some meat or fish left-overs when fishing in her territory. When I caught a fish, I would give her some of what I had brought along, and she wasn't too disappointed. But she never lost her preference for a live fish.

One day when I was fishing in the Side of Leccy a friend came along Kettlewell Lane and called to me. I went up the bank, and we chatted over the wall. My friend, who was facing the water, suddenly broke off in mid-sentence:

148

'What's that cat up to?'

Minnie was running backwards and forwards along the bank, and I could see my rod tip was down in the water. I rushed back, but the fish was gone. My friend was amazed that Minnie knew I had a fish on. He didn't know Minnie! I once caught a half-pound roach in that same place, and put it into the keep-net. Minnie had seen me catch it, and I had given her some tit-bit to keep her happy.She knew the fish was there, in the net, so I was puzzled when she suddenly jumped up and began hopping about as if a fish was in the offing. My float wasn't moving, and I was sure I hadn't missed a bite. Minnie was concentrating on the keep-net and, as I looked, I saw the peg holding it moving downwards. The net was being dragged away, into the water! I pulled it out to find the roach had a gash along one side. A pike had got at it through the net and was trying to make off with it.

Most anglers under-estimated Minnie. When she was with me I would often give my line a tug, making the float bob, and she would jump up immediately. Even when the water surface was very still, and a nibble made rings appear, she would creep to the edge, excited.

Minnie was still around years after the war, and before she disappeared she was for a while accompanied by one of her offspring, a genial tomcat. Although not quite as gifted as his mother, he too was imbued with the local fish culture and devoured many a fish that wasn't meant for him.

Mystery Man

It was as I got to the end of Harewood Parade that I noticed the stranger. He was fishing from the other side, level with the fence that jutted out there. His top joint rested on the lowest rung of the fence, and his float was only inches from the edge. Even young anglers sitting on the fence, would be further out than this man's float. The man was lying along the bank, his head not much more than a foot from his float. On the bank was a large fishing basket, a keep net and landing net. His float was celluloid and lying almost flat, but there was no way of telling where his bait was; it might have been just below his float, only inches out or, if he had a twelve foot depth, it might be almost in the middle at that part of the pond. The float was dipping slightly all the time, so I assumed his bait was being nibbled by tiddlers. Normally I would have asked an angler if he had had any bites, but this man was concentrating so closely that I didn't like to disturb him.

I went along to the Lines and had been fishing only a few minutes when Tom Mitchley came up.

'Funny bloke fishing in the pond! Only a few inches from the side!' I said I had seen him, lying right along the edge. 'He'll get rheumatism if he's not careful!' said Tom.

Two hours later I was trying in the Square when Mr Pegg came over. 'Seen that bloke over there? His float's right at the side, but I suppose his bait could be a fair way out.' I asked if the man was still having a nibble. 'That he is,' said Mr Pegg, 'but it's only tiddlers. Tom says he hasn't looked at his bait for over two hours.'

When I packed up at midday the man was still there, in the same position, apparently having the same nibble. Three men and a couple of boys stood watching. At the Loke end I met Eppy who said he'd seen the man there at half past seven that morning lying in the same position. His float had been in the same place and was dipping slightly all the time.

During the afternoon the stranger had more spectators than would usually stop to see a big'un landed. Still he didn't move from his lying position, still he didn't pull out to look at his bait, and still he had the nibble. Lots of young anglers were discussing him and, when I left at half past five, scores of passers-by had stopped to watch.

That evening I ate as quickly as possible, telling Mr and Mrs Peckover about our stranger, and describing his tackle and how he was fishing. Mr Peckover thought he must be a 'proper' angler.

When I got back to the pond that evening, Messrs Tunmore, Remington and Billman were standing on the turning circle in earnest conversation, glancing frequently at the far end where there were spectators on both banks. The man was in exactly the same position, and had still not pulled in. When I asked if anyone knew what he was using for bait, Mr Remington said:

'I reckon he's using a night gobbler! It's moving around all the time, and that's where his nibble comes from!'

The three men staggered about the turning circle, laughing. Eventually Mr Billman said 'But blast! A bite can't last all day! And you can't fish all day without moving or pulling out! It ain't natural!'

Mr Tunmore said: 'It's not really a bite. He's got a bit of line tied to the hook, and he's holding the other end, twiddling it about.' Again the three neighbours roared with laughter.

Mr Billman said: 'I bet he's got the bit of line tied to a shirt button and that bite's his heart beat!'

Again the three men were helpless with laughter. They watched, still chuckling, as I baited up and went off. The man's float was still quivering as I went behind him, round the end of the pond and cast out from opposite the Tunmores' house. From there I could keep an eye on our stranger. For some time there were guffaws from the turning circle, but at last the neighbours separated. As Mr Tunmore reached his gate he stood looking around at the man and his spectators, glanced over towards me, shrugged his shoulders and went indoors.

As it grew darker, fewer passers-by stopped and more anglers packed up. Eventually only the stranger and I were left, and it was so dark that he was barely visible. Several times I thought of strolling round to talk to the man, but it was too late to start now. I thought it must be ten o'clock - the time I usually got back so that we could have some supper and Mr Peckover could get to bed in reasonable time for his early start the next morning. I waited a few more minutes, then pulled in and packed my things away. There was still no movement from the other side. I climbed slowly over the railings, went through the allotments gate and walked twenty yards along the path. Then I stopped and crept quietly back to the gate and peeped round the hedge. He was still there. I crept away and, half-way through the allotments, broke into a run.

Mrs Peckover was worried, as I knew she would be.

'We wondered where you'd got to! It's after half past ten! Mr Peckover's out looking for you!'

My host returned a few minutes later. 'You didn't come back along the Loke, I know!'

I explained that I had come back through the allotments, and why I was so late. Mr Peckover said:

'I looked everywhere. Went round the Lily Pond, called out along the railway lines..'

'But did you go round the Long Pond itself?'

'Course I did! That's where I thought you'd be.'

'Did you see that man there, along the edge?'

'Didn't see anyone!'

'You must have missed him in the dark. He was by the end of the fence over on the Tunmores' side.'

'I know where he *was*. You told us. I was going to ask him if he'd seen you, but there was nobody there. I looked all round with my torch.'

I half expected to see the man there the next morning. He wasn't. He had fished a whole day without changing his position, without changing his bait and without pulling in. He hadn't had a bite all day long and had fished closer to the side than anyone had done before. Quite a record! We never found out what his bait had been because he never came back.

Lend a Hand on the Land

When the 'Lend a Hand on the Land' project came along almost the whole of our form volunteered, mainly because we would be paid. Early each morning we caught a bus from the Fleet and were taken to Robinson's farm near Tilney All Saints. After my experience in the school garden I thought picking strawberries would be easy. But it wasn't. The second day I could hardly bend down, yet the 'old' women picked furiously all day with the shortest of lunch breaks. The third day I found my preferred method: lying in the straw

151

between rows and picking from that position. That way I could keep going all day. The gangers' favourite cry was:

'Donyoujamarnem!' (Don't you jam on them!)

Owing to a misunderstanding I was under the impression for some days that the men's toilet was in a corner, outside, between a large hut and a smaller one. Once, after I had been there, Jimmy Norton came up unable to contain his laughter. The real toilet was the small hut. Jimmy had gone there and, not able to open the door, had looked through a knot-hole to see if anyone was inside. There was: a local girl who was sitting down peeping through another knot-hole on the other side at me weeing.

Everything we picked was weighed and we were given tokens: cardboard coins with a metal edge. At the end of our two weeks we cashed these in. I managed to earn about four pounds and, as I collected it, realised I had never before had so much money all at once.

Some of us, Linnets and Londoners, later worked on local farms mainly in the North Wootton area. Never very fast, I was often still trying to fill a sack when the others had finished and gone off. I would have to rush to fill my bag and run all the way to North Wootton station, as often as not still a quarter a mile away as the train pulled out along the embankment.

Not many years later I decided to go into teaching and arranged to spend a two-week practice period in Gaywood Park Boys' School. Only a week before this was to start, I ripped my only pair of trousers on some barbed wire at the Square. Mrs Peckover sewed them up for me on the condition that I buy a new pair for the school visit. The next morning, in the patched-up trousers, I went along to the Fleet and caught a bus taking people to local farms. By pure chance I found myself at Tilney All Saints and managed to earn enough to buy a new pair of trousers. When I got to Gaywood Park School I met up with some of the wartime young anglers. including Robert Rose, who were still at school and now about fourteen or fifteen years of age. They were very well-behaved in my lessons, mainly, I think, because their mothers had told them to be.

Paradise Lost

It had been raining hard for several hours and was just leaving off. Along the cul-de-sac was the familiar pattern of puddles, some reaching out from the gutter nearly to the middle of the road. I knew that run-off water would be pouring into the Long Pond, and since there wasn't time to go fishing before the next meal I decided to go out and look around.

The Gaywood River was high, coloured, and flowing strongly under the Swan Laundry bridge. The fish would be on the feed. At the Lines, water swirled from the wide pipe with more force than usual and small fish were

152

breaking the surface. In the Square the water was just over the top of the baffle walls, piling up at the tunnel even more than usual. Where it came out into the pond just the other side of the railway were complicated current patterns half hidden by vapour. In spite of the thick vapour you could still see shoals of small fish moving about in the silvery green water.

I went over the Loke to watch water flowing in through the pipe under the road. In the strong current were hundreds of tiddlers, some at the surface and others lower down taking the full force of the water. A few feet away, in shallow water at the very edge of the pond, shoals of large roach moved swiftly along. What an incredible place the Long Pond was!

I walked to the end of Smith Avenue where we caught large carp and tench. From where I stood you could hear water flowing out at the far end by Peck's Field, so I went along to see what that looked like. Here was a concrete chamber about four feet square, very near the side. The top was barred so that water could flow over the chamber between the bars and away via a pipe into the stream along Peck's Field. In spring, frog and toad spawn found its way into the chamber, then through the pipe into the Peck's Field stream where most of it seemed to hatch out all right. But we did rescue a lot of spawn from inside the chamber and put it back into the Lily Pond, fixing it between plant growth or under banks. Water also flowed into the chamber through a hole at the bottom, and large carp, roach and pike sometimes entered there and got trapped inside. We rescued these also by pushing a landing net down between the bars and sweeping it round. It was rather like catching tiddlers. Fortunately the bars were far enough apart to allow even the largest carp and pike to be pulled through if they were held in an upright position.

What a paradise the Long Pond was!

I wandered round the far end of the Lily Pond and along the other side back to the Loke. The shoals of large roach were still there, although they moved away as I passed. The tiddlers in the current would take a lot more disturbing and were reluctant to leave the moving water even if you waded almost to the ledge just above the pipe.

As I reached the Loke Road pavement, Mrs Rose, David and Robert, were leaving Froes' carrying shopping bags. The Froes had a stall in the yard in front of their house in Loke Road and sold vegetables. We all crossed the road together, Mrs Rose asking me how my hosts were, and the boys asking her if they could come fishing with me later on. When they had gone indoors I walked along the shallow end of the Long Pond and stood looking towards the Point. Homesick as always, I nevertheless felt overwhelmed by the beauty of it all. Even with houses all around there was still clean water supporting all this natural life. Could there possibly be anywhere else like it? But then came a disturbing thought: was this all too good to last? Fish, completely dependent

153

Looking towards the Point on a washing day

on water, were so vulnerable. So many things could spoil it all. Look what had happened to many rivers in the north because of industrialisation. Look what had happened to My Ditch. I stared along the pond, shutting my eyes then opening them, trying to see it all afresh, determined to appreciate everything while it was still there.

Over a year later, during the summer holidays, a few of us were fishing between the Point and the railway end. It was a very hot afternoon and the fish were not biting. A game of cricket was going on. The ball had landed out in the middle several times and been retrieved by our stone-throwing method. It was Laurie (Lodge) Wakefield, not a regular angler, who came running up from the Loke direction.

'Quick! Lots of fish dying at the end!'

We sprinted after him. Dorsal fins of carp were showing above the surface in the shallow water. Lots of smaller fish were lying on their sides, moving but not able to keep upright. We rushed back for our landing nets and eight or ten of us began netting fish out. All we could do was carry them in our nets over the road and put them into the Lily Pond. We did this feverishly for the rest of the afternoon, taking carp, roach, bream, gudgeon, dace and one or two pike to the other side. We must have transferred hundreds of fish. Most of them seemed to revive and only four or five lay there looking as if they would not recover. For the first hour or so we seemed to be getting nowhere because more fish came crowding into the shallow water all the time, but we gradually had fewer and fewer to deal with, until finally there were no more visible. We decided that the electric light works must have put out hotter water, or more of it than usual. That and the hot weather combined to raise the water temperature and lower the oxygen content. Fortunately the Lily Pond had not been affected so much; its water felt distinctly cooler to the touch. We stood there for some time, deciding what we might do to prevent it happening again. As we stood there I realised that we were in exactly the same place as when, over a year earlier, I had feared it might all be too good to last. Also we had just crossed the road scores of times with sick fish, exactly where I had crossed with Mrs Rose and her two boys all that time ago. Was this the beginning of a confirmation of my fears?

The others, having rescued so many fish and seen them revive, were feeling happier, even elated, and thought the combination of hot water and hot weather was not likely to happen again. But the coincidence was so striking that I was not optimistic.

We had to rescue fish the next summer, and twice the following summer.

⊷⊪⊫⊪⊷

Although small, the Square had three parts to it: a rectangle where the water rushed in from the electric light works, a very narrow strip between the two baffle walls, and the largest part, a parallelogram, bounded on one side by the railway. I had decided to fish in the Square that day and, walking through the allotments, I wondered which part to fish in. The day before, I had seen several large carp move into the rectangular part from the direction of the electric light works, so decided to try there first. I climbed the fence and crept carefully over the single railway line trying not to disturb the fish.

There was something different, but it wasn't until I saw the water that I knew what it was. There was no sound of water rushing from the Leccy Pit down the steep pipe. For the first time I was looking down at still water in the Square. No water swirled into the rectangular part, no water rushed and twisted between the baffle walls, and no water was piling up at the tunnel under the railway.

From that day onwards the electric light works no longer produced electricity for twenty-four hours every day because electricity was being produced elsewhere. So, for some of the time the water in the Square was still. No water flowed under Loke Road into the Lily Pond making the current the tiddlers loved, and no water flowed through the chamber at the far end. Water didn't rush through the pipe from the Long Pond and come out at the Lines. There was slow movement at the Saunders as water went along the Gaywood River, but no water poured through any of the mysterious tunnels, and both Side and Back of Leccy were almost motionless. The places worst hit were the Square, Lines and Lily Pond because it was the strong current that had made them what they were. When the water was still, there was less depth, and the bottom was visible, but there were no fish to be seen.

155

The Lily Pond in 1996

One day I was fishing in that rectangular part of the Square when the water wasn't moving. The water was low and the bottom visible. It looked dead. Then the electric light works started up and the water began moving, slowly at first, then strongly. Within minutes small fish were jumping and breaking the surface. I had a big bite, and missed it. Things were back for a while to what they had been.

This change took place quite late during the war, yet the days of the current working all day and all night were soon forgotten. Many young anglers who fished then don't remember them.

Re-evacuated

We thought it was going to be another ordinary school day, and walked from the classroom, along the passage, out through the back door, past the bike shed and into the small hall where assembly was held. We had done it every school day for years. But the announcement was totally unexpected. Our teachers were all returning to London and the school was to close. We were strongly advised to be re-evacuated and join a London school in Bury St Edmunds. Already, as we walked away, most of my classmates were saying there was no point in being re-evacuated at the age of fifteen or sixteen. The school was closing because the classes had become so small. Our own form had varied between six and a dozen, and the other forms were not much bigger.

For a while I didn't believe it would happen; the war had been littered with changes of plan, and I waited for this one to change. But as the date drew near it became obvious that the school would indeed close. Some Lynn friends urged me to stay and go to a Lynn school, but there were difficulties. If I had been going home it would not have been so bad, but going to another place and leaving all the fish and Lynn friends would be sad. The thought of leaving the Long Pond was the saddest one of all. But as the leaving date drew nearer I began to be more optimistic. Didn't everything happen for the best? Lynn had been a strange place at first, yet it had turned out to have the Long Pond and lots of nice people. Why shouldn't Bury St Edmunds turn out to be the same?

The day arrived. As Mr Peckover went off to work he shook my hand and wished me the best of luck. Mrs Reddy came in from next door and did the same. I had collected together some of my belongings and fishing tackle, but my bedroom was still full of treasures I couldn't possibly carry. My hosts told me my room would always be available whenever I wanted it.

Mrs Peckover came with me to the station, and as we carried the luggage past the Long Pond I looked around at the familiar parts of the bank, the water and the houses. I knew I would have to come back.

Jimmy Norton was the only other person from my form being evacuated. There were about a dozen of us, and one teacher. The only thing I remember about the journey was that we stopped at a station and one of our group must have opened a carriage door on the wrong side. A railwayman stormed in and told us we'd have the door off.

As soon as we arrived at Bury St Edmunds our teacher went off to catch a London train, and we were taken away in a search for billets. There was refusal after refusal, and only occasionally was somebody persuaded to take one of us in. It was early evening when I saw the last of the others billeted, but I was still left. Some time later I was handed over to a man and a lady who had a car, and was driven around in the search for a billet. We called at dozens of houses, and it was late in the evening when we came to a narrow street with small houses on each side. I stayed in the car while the man and lady knocked at a door and went inside. It was a long time before they came out, saying they had found me a place. They helped me in with my luggage and drove away. I was alone with my new hosts. They explained that they hadn't wanted an evacuee because they were too old, and neither was very well. They produced some sandwiches, but I could have eaten four times that amount. The man showed me into a small bedroom and, to forget my hunger, I decided to go to bed immediately.

After what seemed like five minutes I was being shaken by the man - who couldn't pronounce my name:

'Ked! Ked! Time to get up!'

He gave me some breakfast. I suspected the lady was still in bed, and that the man was not usually up at that time either.

I hadn't the faintest idea where the school was, and it took me a long time to find it. I joined Jimmy Norton and a small group of seniors who were with the headmaster. We were with him all day, and lessons consisted of a bit of chat and being left to our own devices the rest of the time. We understood from the others that this was the usual routine. I asked the head about fishing in the area, but he had no idea, and gave me the name of a boy in the school who was a keen angler. I found the boy, and he told me all about the local fishing. There were no carp, and the fish he described would, in Lynn, have been classed as little'uns. This wasn't a great disappointment because already I couldn't bear the thought of using my tackle in a strange place.

By that afternoon Jimmy Norton and I had discovered that all the classes were smaller than ours had been in Lynn, and that there were fewer pupils in the school as a whole. Why hadn't this school been evacuated to us?

As we were coming out of school I realised I didn't know my new address. I thought it might be Bishop's Road, but wasn't at all sure. There was plenty of time, so I decided to walk around and explore before trying to find my new billet. Half an hour later I came across a quiet road with a stream running under it. I looked at the downstream side for some time, but saw no living creature, so crossed the road and looked over railings at the other side.

There, just below, was a leech. At first it seemed to be fighting a losing battle against the current, and was almost swept out of sight below where I was standing. But it managed to catch hold of something and, by stretching and contracting, made headway upstream. Several times it was forced backwards again, but each time succeeded in holding on to something and advancing again. Eventually it wriggled into a calm place near the side, and went down out of sight.

The leech seemed to have known what it wanted and, as I walked away, I suddenly knew what I wanted as well. I went to the station and asked the price of a single ticket to London.

My hosts' faces lit up when I told them I was leaving, and they were only too pleased to lend me two shillings and tenpence to make up the price of my journey to King's Cross.

The last evening in Bishop's Road was a very pleasant one. My hosts, until then depressed, silent and morose, were transformed into a friendly, smiling and talkative couple. They asked me a lot of questions, and told me about themselves. The lady even said she had been a very beautiful woman when she was young. I said 'Really?', realised it was the wrong thing to say, and tried to play down my surprise.

My second evacuation had been very different from the first. There had been only about a dozen of us. The one teacher had promptly left us for London. We had been met by only two or three people, and no crowds cheered. Instead of being the first to find a billet I had been the last. My hosts hadn't wanted an evacuee. I had stayed only three days, spent one day at school, and wrote no letter home.

And there had been no Long Pond.

Lynn News & Advertiser, Summer, 1975

Action on puzzle of dead fish

AN investigation has begun to solve the puzzle of why fish up to four pounds in weight have died in local waters.

Two hundred roach may have perished in the Mill Basin at Tilney-cum-Islington probably because of lack of oxygen, while other varieties have been taken from the Long Pond which crosses under Lynn's Loke Road.

Fish from both spots are being analysed. Carrying out the analysis are scientists from the Anglian Water Authority who are also looking at water samples.

Early indications are that it is lack of oxygen which is causing the deaths but pollution has not been ruled out.

If pollution is discovered the water authority has promised to trace the source.

Residents near the Long Pond have been concerned for some time about its overgrown and dirty state and raised the alarm on Tuesday when they spotted dead fish floating.

They contacted Mr Robin Goldsmith of 8 Raby Avenue who told his employers, the water authority.

Pump

A pump moved fresh water from the Gaywood river into the pond to improve the survival chances of the remaining fish.

Among the fish scooped out by children were carp, pike, roach and rudd.

West Norfolk Council has received complaints that the pond has become overgrown, dirty, cluttered with rubbish and an attraction to rats.

Mrs Pamela Mitchelson of 2 Townshend Terrace, which fronts on to the pond told the LN & A: "The pond smells terrible at night time. It used to be lovely. The children have tried to clear it themselves to fish."

Mr Ken Faulkner, the council's public relations officer said: "We are going to take action in the very near future to clean it up."

The Mill Basin, responsibility of the Marshland Smeeth and Fen Internal Drainage Board, is to be dredged next year, said Mr David Tester, the water authority's principal quality officer for the Great Ouse Division.

Weed

At present the surface is covered with a thick layer of weed making the counting of the dead fish difficult.

Mr Tester said: "If we find that there is any obvious sign of pollution from an outside source we will take action to stop it."

But early indications are that death is due to lack of oxygen which is, he said, "very low in the water".

Historic ponds to be preserved

LNA 19/1/82

Members and officers from West Norfolk council met the public and plan the future of the Long Ponds. (82/234).

THE FUTURE of Lynn's historic Long Ponds now looks assured, and work to improve their appearance could get underway in the spring.

That was the outcome of a site visit to the ponds, situated off Loke Road, by members and officers of West Norfolk council, on Friday.

After touring the area and speaking to local residents, the councillors rejected any suggestion that the ponds should be filled in and turned into play areas.

"We are unanimously of the opinion that the Long Ponds should be preserved as an historical water feature," said leisure and tourism services committee chairman Mr Leslie Dutton.

"The purpose of our site visit is to look at ways of preserving them as an attractive amenity for the people of Lynn.

"Some areas around the ponds are still attractive, and others can be made so. We are encouraged by the fact that most local residents want to see them remain as waterways.

"We will now start looking at detailed proposals for improving the ponds and

look to include some financial provision for the project in our financial estimates for the next financial year.

"The environmental services committee might also have a part to play in things, and we may be able to get the Manpower Services Commission interested in a 'Youth' Opportunities' Programme.

"I would hope that some work could begin in the spring," said Mr Dutton.

Harewood Parade resident Mrs Jane Thomas said she hoped the council wouldn't decide to fill in the Long Ponds.

"If they did that and then landscaped them, people would still throw their rubbish in. At least if they keep the water level up high, the

stuff will sink out of sight and there won't be a smell in summer time," said Mrs Thomas.

However, Mrs Angela Hamer, of Smith Avenue, said she would like to see the Long Ponds drained and filled in because they were an attraction to vandals and in danger to children.

"I have got two small children and I have to keep a constant eye on them in case they go near the ponds, which are not fenced off," she told the Lynn News.

The Long Ponds once formed an outer feature of the old town walls of the borough of Lynn and have also been used as an overflow cooling device for the former electricity generating station located nearby.

The Long Pond Area Today

The Square, Leccy Pit, Side of Leccy, Back of Leccy and parts of Saunders (flotsam bin, tunnel, sluice gate area) have all been filled in. The Lily Pond has been narrowed; so has the lower Long Pond, where the Boards used to be along the the north west bank.The smaller ditches have either been filled in or are dry or polluted and contain no water life. The Gaywood River has a high nitrate content, so there is little weed that gives cover, but there are still some fish there. The river is generally narrower and lower than in 1939. The northern bank where, during the war and for some time after, there was a path to the bridge in Wootton Road, is no longer open to the public.

The pipes under Loke Road and between the Long Pond and the Lines Bridge remain. The latter is now used for pumping water in the opposite direction (from Gaywood River to the Long Ponds) at times of low water or insufficient oxygen in the ponds.

Epilogue

Not many years ago, in the East End of London where I was evacuated from, the Gatehouse School had a system of collecting rainwater from roofs and circulating it through classrooms in transparent pipes. The idea was to bring the sight and sound of water to children who hardly ever experienced such a thing. This was well after the war, when new buildings, roads and pavements had mostly replaced the old ones.

Before the war we were not so deprived. Rainwater came from roofs through down-pipes, across pavements into deep gutters. We could float matchsticks a long way in these before coming to a drain. And there were puddles in irregular surfaces all over roads and pavements.

There were plenty of gutters and puddles in the Lynn of 1939. There were also ditches, dykes, streams, rivers and ponds. We not only saw and heard water, we could also smell and touch it. What's more, plants, insects and fish flourished there. My wartime hosts saw roach, gudgeon, pike and eels when out for a Sunday stroll. Local allotment holders and gardeners saw sticklebacks, tadpoles, eels and brook pike when they fetched a bucket of water from a nearby river, pond, dyke or ditch. In the small dyke where Columbia Way now runs, there were large eels - as the workers discovered during the digging-out prior to in-filling.

Norfolk avoided the water pollution of the industrial revolution, but not the pollution, lowering of water tables and 'development' that began in earnest during the 1950s. Even in the 1940s we watched dismayed as water, where shoals of fish used to swim, receded or dried up. At one time we could only just get a float under the highest part of the Swan Laundry Bridge. Not long ago I saw boys on rafts go under that bridge without having to duck their heads.

Streams in the Chase and Hardwick Road areas used to be over three feet deep, and held enough fish to support otters. That has all gone.

Without realising it, many people now walk, cycle or drive over what was pure water in 1939. But the elimination of water has been going on for a long time. When in 1939 we went around the Long Ponds, along Blackfriars Road, Austin Street, the recreation ground and even parts of Loke Road itself, we also did not know that we were over places that had before been pure water. When we fished (and trespassed) in the electric light works area, or roamed the other side of that building, we had no idea there had been water where we saw dry land.

The lower reaches of the Gaywood and Nar Rivers now have such a high nitrate content that there is no proper weed cover for the fish that remain. For years, beginning in 1960, Neville Tunmore and I tried to persuade the Great Ouse River Authority to do something about pollution, extraction and low water levels, but they would never agree that there was anything wrong.

Lynn is not unique. All over Britain thousands of village ponds, cattle-watering places, lakes, rivers, streams and road-side ditches have been polluted, drained, filled in or rendered invisible by being piped underground. The same process has been happening all over the world. On every continent, local wells and ponds have disappeared because of projects like dams, reservoirs and canalisation - perhaps in distant places, where large populations have been rendered homeless.

In Britain not long ago, water could be seen almost everywhere in ditches, streams, ponds and meandering rivers. It was small-scale, unchanging and permanent. And it was essentially 'local'. As late as the 1960s Wilfred Peckover regularly scraped out a hollow in the bed of the dyke so that he could collect buckets of water more easily. Mr Goldsmith, an elderly tenant in Mill Houses, had a part-time water job. He kept a stretch of the Gaywood River clear of surplus water-weed using a dung fork (the tines at 90 degrees) tied to a length of rope. He also raised and lowered the Saunders sluice (and glowered at us for trespassing there). There were also the Dutch families who maintained parts of the Great Ouse banks.

Nobody claims that pollution, low water levels and the elimination of water are good things in themselves. These results have never been deliberate policy. So why have they come about? This question cannot be answered here, but any answer has to do with the way societies change from one kind of system to another.* As far as water is concerned the earlier system is when local people are all acquainted with the same stretches of water, have similar knowledge and beliefs about them and the forms of life they support, have a close relationship with them, and depend on local wells and springs for most or all of their water. Local water and its contents play, at this stage, an important part in the economics, politics, religion, socialisation, education and entertainment activities of the group.

In the later system, people know little or nothing about local water, mainly because there isn't any. The local water that does exist is known about only by those with special knowledge or interests; we can include anglers amongst these. But they are more likely to be interested only in stretches of water elsewhere, perhaps in other countries. If there are sticklebacks, loach, gudgeon or small eels in a local brook, they are unlikely to attract the attention of local anglers who will only be interested in one or two particular species of fish (probably large) in other parts of the world. Anglers mix with other specialist anglers from elsewhere. The angling groups that spring up consist of individuals from distant and different areas with only one interest in common. Their angling is not something to do with the local economy, politics, religion, socialisation, education or entertainment. It is to do with a special kind of activity that brings people together from disparate populations. So instead of fishing in a spare half hour just down the lane,

*See the types of society as analysed by, for example, Emile Durkheim, Ferdinand Tönnies or Herbert Spencer.

164

over a field or from the back garden, anglers now travel long distances by car or plane for longer sessions in the Americas, Africa, Asia or the Antipodes. The rest of the population knows little or nothing about fish or fishing. Anglers form a specialist group, a much smaller fraction of the population than in the past, when people fished locally. Not surprisingly, with the expense and time involved, children tend not to go fishing, and it becomes a problem for the angling groups to recruit enough young people into their ranks.

As for water itself, it is no longer everywhere in small amounts. It is in fewer places, but in larger quantities, and for specific purposes: drinking, fishing, sailing, swimming etc. Ponds, lakes or other fishing waters come into existence suddenly in new places and for particular kinds of fish. This water is maintained by specialists, has to be re-stocked regularly, and anglers pay to fish there. The fish are bred elsewhere, and transported. It becomes less and less common for fish to be born, to mature, breed and die in the same water.

All this is usually seen in an optimistic light by those involved. Anglers see ponds coming back. More people have ponds in their gardens. Fish are reared, and garden ponds might contain fish worth thousands of pounds. With the consent and advice of the Environment Agency we can construct ponds and lakes where, before, there was no water to be seen. We have Conservation Advisers who can tell us where and how to excavate, what fish to introduce, and which insects and plants we should invest in. The catchword is 'biodiversity'. But of course we had indigenous biodiversity before. And these new enterprises are not likely to impinge on the lives of most people especially the young, elderly and poor, except to make their water scarcer and more expensive than before. The new water cannot become local, communal, unchanging, permanent, self-sufficient or need minimum upkeep. It is private and for special purposes and groups. It can't bring back the local sticklebacks, tadpoles, 'fat ol' tench' or the mysterious monster in the village's bottomless pond.

In Lynn now, the Square, Leccy Pit, Side and Back of Leccy, the Horseshoe Pond and almost all the small ditches have gone. The Long Pond is isolated except for an occasional input of nitrate-laden water from a narrower and shallower Gaywood River. For reasons of heritage the Long Pond and Lily Pond have been saved. The fact that they are still there means that the people in that part of Lynn are comparatively fortunate.

✦✦✦✦✦✦